D1077275

New Product Development

An introduction to a multifunctional process

Tim Jones

Butterworth-Heinemann
Linacre House, Jordan Hill, Oxford OX2 8DP
A division of Reed Educational and Professional Publishing Ltd

℞   A member of the Reed Elsevier plc group

OXFORD   BOSTON   JOHANNESBURG
MELBOURNE   NEW DELHI   SINGAPORE

First published 1997

© Tim Jones 1997

British Library Cataloguing in Publication Data
A catalogue record for this book is
available from the British Library

ISBN 0 7506 2427 2

Composition by Genesis Typesetting, Rochester, Kent
Printed and bound in Great Britain by Biddles Ltd, Guildford and
King's Lynn

Contents

ch 1.

Preface

The successful development of new products has become a complex process involving contributions from a range of different disciplines. Rarely is one individual responsible for the conception, design, development, manufacture and marketing of a new product, for today the inherent complexity of products, their markets and therefore the processes through which they are developed, dictates that a number of different people, each with their own roles, work together to create the product. Scientists, designers, engineers and marketeers form the core of new product development and they are in turn supported by management, purchasing, finance and quality personnel.

This book presents a cross-disciplinary discussion of new product development, its organization, its management, the key stages, the key functions involved and their mutual interactions. It addresses the various issues associated with the development of new products and details the process through which they are developed. It outlines the roles and responsibilities of each discipline and puts each into context as individual but inter-related parts of the whole process and details how, only when they are all working together, successful products are more efficiently developed. Through the use of several case studies, it goes on to demonstrate how a number of selected manufacturers have successfully integrated the separate elements into the new product development process and, in each case, identifies and emphasizes the points highlighted by each company.

The book has been written to be relevant to anyone involved in new product development: designers, engineers, marketing personnel and managers. It is intended to both explain the issues present in new product development and indicate how each function has a role and how they all interact during the development process. It is not meant to cover every aspect of every type of new product development programme, but rather to give an accessible account of the approach that is currently being taken in leading manufacturing companies. It is hoped that, through reading this book, readers will gain an understanding of not only their own but also each other's roles in the development of new products and appreciate the advantages of working together to create the new products upon which the country's future economic prosperity depends.

Tim Jones

Acknowledgements

I would like to thank a number of key individuals for their cooperation in the production of this book. These include Anne Youngson, David Halliwell and Kevin Jones at Rover; John Coathupe, Helen Pocock and Brian Wytcherley at Flymo; Kieran Devey and Frank Morley at Logitech and Paul Fearis at PDD who have all provided significant input to the case studies. In addition I would also like to thank Rachel Cooper, John Sanger and Henry Waters at Salford for their support throughout the compilation of the text.

Introduction

The new product development (NPD) process is in a state of constant change. As new organizational structures are adopted, new technology becomes available and product development strategies are redefined, the core process itself is continually being modified to embrace and accommodate these changes. As manufacturers seek to produce more innovative products, reduce development periods, decrease development costs, and improve the quality of both the product and the process, many are now moving into second or third generation processes where identifiable and discrete stages are being replaced by more flexible schedules within parallel programmes.

Considerable variation exists in the processes adopted by different sectors and different companies, so an individual product may demand a modified process for its development, sometimes through the need to incorporate new technology and sometimes to meet specific market requirements. Despite these variations the development process has been frequently modelled to explain the various stages and help organizations plan product development more effectively. Some of these models have addressed the marketing orientated stages, some the core design phases whilst others have provided a general perspective. However there is an overall framework of the development process emerging onto which most development programmes can be mapped and it is this which provides the basis of this book.

The NPD process (Figure I.1) can be split into three distinct phases each of which is itself composed of a number of component stages:

- the *inception* phase covers the pre-development activities which are undertaken before a product concept is even visualized,
- the *creation* phase includes the core development stages associated with generating a product concept and taking it through to a working prototype, whilst
- the *realization* phase deals with taking the final design, putting it into manufacture and launching it onto the market.

Each of these three phases have their own characteristics, requirements and contributors and each demands individual management and control. In

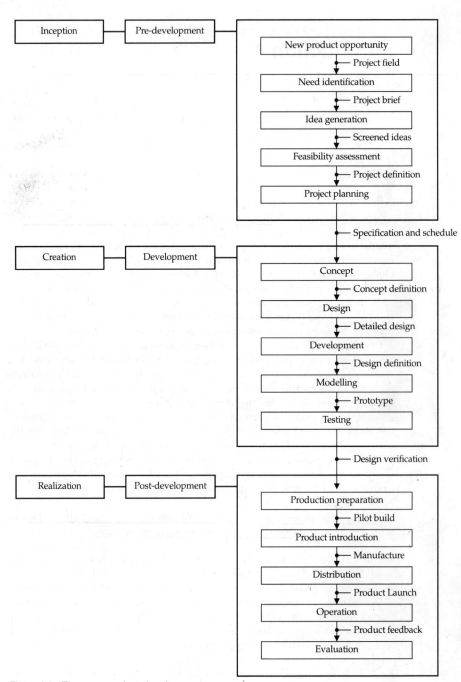

Figure I.1   The new product development process

addition each phase and component stages have their own specific and identifiable outcomes which in turn enable the effective undertaking of the subsequent stage or phase.

Whilst historically each stage has been the responsibility of an individual function, as explained in Chapter 3, it is now common for the varied functions associated with a contemporary product development project to be involved throughout the process (Figure I.2). Although at certain points this involvement may well be only in a consultative capacity, as a typical project progresses, all of the key functions become active participants and frequently take the lead role for a period.

During the inception phase, it is primarily market research and research and development which take the major roles. Together with marketing, design and senior management, a new product opportunity is initially examined and, if appropriate to the organization, its technological capabilities and the market, a specific project field is identified. The area for a new product thus defined, with assistance from sales and product support, the needs of both users and stake-holders are next determined and subsequently assessed against key market, technology and business requirements. Should the project field prove to be valid for development, an initial brief describing the overall area and requirements can then be compiled. Although in no way definitive at this stage, such a document can nevertheless begin to identify the key problems likely to be encountered, the product opportunities and also give an indication of the potential market and users. With the scope of the project clarified, the idea generation stage follows, typically led by research and development with the active participation of marketing and design and the support of other NPD functions. Once a range of ideas have been generated and perhaps initially screened, the majority of functions next participate in an assessment of their feasibility. Across the group, the ideas are assessed not only against market and technology parameters, but also with respect to synergy with the business. From this the most promising idea or ideas can be selected using agreed product criteria and the project defined. ¡Only at this point, once all this pre-development investigation and analysis has been undertaken, can the development of a product be planned and a product specification compiled.

The central creation phase is usually largely led by design. Although benefiting from the active participation of some other functions and regularly consulting with the rest, it is the primary role of design to conceive a range of product concepts, select the most appropriate and develop them through to prototype stage. The development of product concepts which answer the specification and address the identified product requirements is commonly an activity dominated by a combination of R&D and design personnel, but as individual concepts are defined and the product itself designed in detail, both production engineering and manufacturing begin to take a more active role in the development programme. Whilst it is typical for the majority of NPD functions to be consulted throughout the creation phase, it is production engineering and manufacturing who are ultimately responsible for realizing the product and therefore projects often profit from

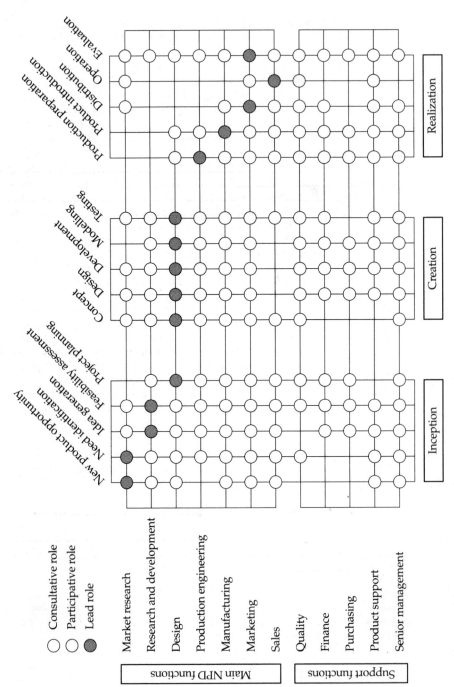

Figure 1.2 Functional involvement during a typical new product development programme

their participation in support of the core design team. However, once a product has been designed and modelled, the number of functions that become actively involved in the testing stage increases considerably. Whilst production engineering and manufacturing clearly need to assess the manufacturability of the developed product, marketing and market research frequently assess not only whether it meets the initially identified needs but, armed with representative and sometimes working models, they can also begin to undertake user clinics and hall test to evaluate customer reactions and product perceptions. As well as assessing whether the developed product satisfies agreed requirements, this also enables key product attributes to be investigated, assessed and, if necessary, refined. It is also at this stage that senior management take an active role in using the results of this testing and supporting market analysis to ascertain product potential and determine whether or not to allow the product to go into production.

The third realization phase, where the product is introduced first to the manufacturing facility and then to the marketplace, is where production engineering, manufacturing and marketing take control of the project. Whilst the transfer of a verified design to the production environment relies on inputs from design as well as production engineering and manufacturing, once pilot build has been completed, design's contribution decreases to be replaced by marketing. In preparation for the launch of the product, they now have a vested interest in how effectively initial manufacture occurs so that, in conjunction with sales, they can oversee distribution and coordinate promotion before final release. During this period an initial input from finance and purchasing in helping to establish an economical and reliable production capability also declines whilst product support begin to take an active role so that they are fully operational at product launch. Thus, once the product is on the market, sales usually take the lead role in the product life-cycle with assistance from marketing, quality and product support. Finally, as part of an ongoing programme of continuous incremental improvement of products, evaluation of the product in use is undertaken so that information can be fed back to the manufacturing facility and the rest of the development team. It is here that market research once again begin to take an active role, working with marketing and sales to measure product performance and determine what problems need to be addressed in subsequent models.

The following chapters give an overview of the aspects of new product development as it occurs today. Chapter 1 addresses the subject of new product development strategies and the thinking that goes behind the initiation of a development programme, whilst Chapter 2 examines some of the factors associated with innovation in new products. Chapter 3 then looks at some of the key organizational issues and lastly, Chapter 4 summarizes influences in achieving rapid product development. The four accompanying case studies of the Rover 600, Flymo Gardenvac, Logitech Mouseman Sensa and Polaroid's latest instant camera all provide detailed examples of how this spectrum of activities has been recently addressed in a number of major development programmes.

1   New product development strategy

Introduction

This first chapter examines the subject of business strategy and specifically manufacturers' strategies for new product development. It discusses corporate objectives, identifies some of the key influences on business strategies from both within and external to the organization. It examines how a number of derivative strategies addressing manufacturing, promotion, resources and product development are generated in order to enable the key business objectives to be met and then looks in more detail at the product development strategy itself. Four types of product strategy are discussed and the means of determining an appropriate product development strategy is addressed. The options of pursuing product development whether independently or in collaboration with others are discussed and an example is detailed. Finally the need for the majority of manufacturers to continually develop new products in order to maintain their market share is discussed and illustrated.

Corporate objectives

All organizations have a central purpose behind their existence. They have a primary reason for making the products, providing the services or staging the events which they undertake as part of their core activities. This central aim or key objective is the *raison d'etre* of the organization and for most successful manufacturers lies at the heart of their business strategy. It is always financially driven with the intention of making money for the company, but is also frequently based on particular ambitions within a product sector or market. Whether it is to become the world's largest airline, Europe's most profitable insurance company or a leading manufacturer of audio equipment, this aim gives rise to a number of corporate objectives relating to the market, technology and the organization's capabilities.

Business strategy

A strategy is a plan, a programme of events or actions designed to achieve something. It determines how identified objectives can be realized by the organization involved. Essentially the business strategy defines where a company is at the present time, where it wants to be at a set point in the future and how it is going to get there.

In determining a business strategy, an organization may conduct an extensive 'SWOT' appraisal of internal strengths and weaknesses and external opportunities and threats (Ansoff, 1987). These can address both the short and long term objectives, may involve assessment of both existing and predicted development scenarios and frequently rely on in-depth research combined with detailed knowledge of prevailing conditions. They enable manufacturers to select the most appropriate markets and define their methods and techniques for addressing them.

Internally such an appraisal may draw upon five areas:

- the organization's assets – its financial and material resources,
- the organization's capabilities – its skills, its manufacturing potential and the services it can provide,
- the organization's product range,
- prevailing conditions in the industrial sector in which it operates and
- the organization's competitive advantages – its ability to add more value than rival manufacturers (Kay, 1993).

We can consider that the business strategy is therefore influenced by a combination of the particular ambitions held by a company and the influences on the organization both from within and from outside. Figure 1.1 summarizes some of the component influences which can therefore be considered as internal drivers on a business strategy. Whilst not all are necessarily applicable to every company, this diagram illustrates the diversity of items which can affect the development of a typical business strategy solely from within an organization. Similarly Figure 1.2 shows a number of external drivers on a business strategy. Issues such as trends in the global economy, demography, consumer lifestyles and key markets, changing customer expectations of products' price, performance and reliability, increasing rates of technological development and redundancy and maturing supplier relationships can all also play a significant role in determining which particular overall business strategy an organization chooses to adopt for its planned future growth.

New product strategy

In association with the evolution of an overall business strategy to achieve their corporate objectives, most manufacturers also develop a number of derivative strategies addressing different facets of the company, each

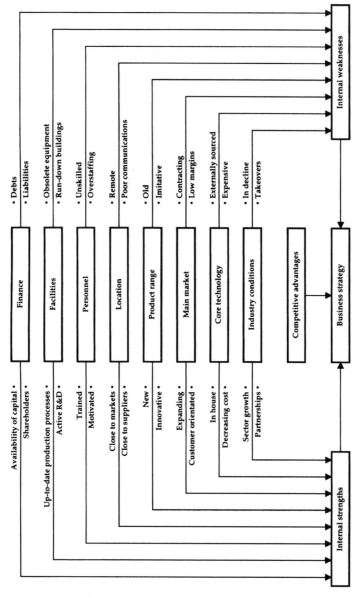

Figure 1.1 Internal drivers on business strategy

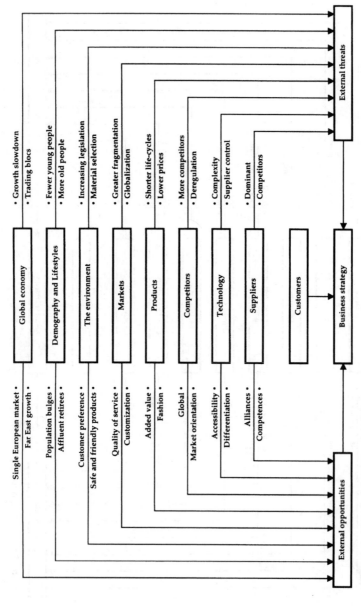

Figure 1.2 External drivers on business strategy

individually contributing to enabling the business strategy to be undertaken. Whilst varying from one organization to another, such derivative strategies (Figure 1.3) may typically be:

- a production strategy addressing the materials, processes and manufacture of existing products,
- a promotion strategy for these products and the organization, dealing with corporate image, public relations and advertising,
- a resource strategy covering issues such as availability of finance and skilled personnel, equipment, facilities and buildings, and
- a new product strategy relating to the type of products to be developed, the markets in which they will be sold, the technology to be incorporated and the resources necessary to develop them.

Although each address separate features of the organization's operations, they are, to a large extent, inter-dependent and collectively provide the course of actions deemed appropriate to fulfil the overall business strategy and meet the identified corporate objectives. Whilst all four are of major significance and have to be addressed within the organization, it is clearly the new product strategy which most directly influences an organization's new product development activities.

Before examining the composition and determination of a new product strategy in more detail, it is appropriate to first consider the different approaches to new product development that can be adopted by manufacturers. Although no two companies will necessarily have either identical objectives or business and new product strategies, there are four generic groups of new product strategy into which most manufacturers can be

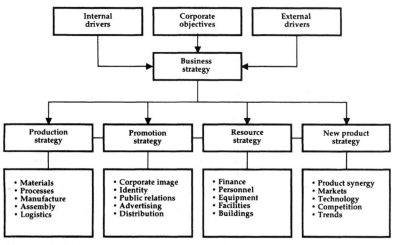

Figure 1.3 Derivative strategies

classified (Freeman, 1982). These are offensive, defensive, imitative and traditional (Table 1.1).

Offensive product development is characterized by significant R&D activity developing new technology and new processes which enable manufacturers to be first to market with innovative new products allowing them to establish an early lead of the field. As the leaders, such organizations are heavily dependent upon the latest information concerning not only technology but also market forecasts, anticipated customer and consumer behaviour as well as economic indications. Although frequently considered high risk because of the uncertainty and levels of investment involved, if a product is successful and is subsequently followed by variants to reinforce market share, this approach can enable early domination of the market which, if built upon, provides the opportunity for long term growth: Pilkington's development and patenting of the float glass production process enabled them to dominate their sector worldwide, Du Pont's successful transfer of Teflon from aerospace to applications ranging from bearings to saucepans has given them access to many new markets, whilst Polaroid's invention of instant film and Hoover's production of vacuum cleaners have both resulted in the two brands becoming synonymous with the respective products.

Defensive product development relies less on developing the original idea, but more on using the company's resources and skills to develop and manufacture improved and competitively priced versions of the product in large volumes in order to gain a share of the follow-on market. This

Table 1.1 Types of new product strategies

Type	Characteristics	Examples
Offensive	● Innovators ● Research intensive ● High risk/uncertainty ● Current information	Pilkington – float glass Du Pont – Teflon Polaroid – instant film Hoover – vacuum cleaners
Defensive	● Followers ● Incremental innovation ● Production quality ● Market focus	Matsushita – VHS video IBM – personal computers WordPerfect – computer software Nissan – cars
Imitative	● Low cost manufacture ● Licensed technology ● No R&D ● Localized markets	Compaq – computers Molson – dry beer Daewoo – cars Samsung – microwave ovens
Traditional	● Established markets ● Constant demand ● Niche market ● Low technology	Barbour – clothing Aga – cookers Zippo – cigarette lighters Mont Blanc – pens

approach relies not on being the first to market with a totally new product, but on being the organization which capitalizes on the technology, process or market. It is less risky than offensive product development as it focuses on existing products, but relies on knowing the market and having the ability to quickly develop new products to satisfy existing consumer demand and meet anticipated short term expectations. One of the best examples of this type of approach in action is Matsushita (Pascale and Athos, 1981) who have refined the production and marketing of improved products to a point where they are the world's largest manufacturer of electrical equipment. Although Ampex and RCA developed the first video recorders for professional use and Sony's Betamax system gained an initial foothold on the the home entertainment market, it was Matsushita's technically inferior but more market focused Panasonic VHS products which quickly dominated the sector. Likewise, the personal computer market established by Radio Shack in the 1970s, became dominated in the 1980s by IBM who used its size, reputation and marketing skills to take over the business market and, in the same sector, Microsoft's Word software for word processing was faster, cheaper, better supported and thus more successful than the preceding WordStar programme. While in the automotive market, where price and quality are both major factors, companies like Nissan have not traditionally developed many new and innovative designs but grown steadily by producing low cost/high reliability alternatives to Ford, GM and Toyota products.

Imitative product development (Schnaars, 1994) is in some ways similar to the defensive approach as it also focuses on the economical production of large volumes of existing types of product but, rather than developing improved versions of original products, this relies more on taking advantage of localized markets and the ability to manufacture products at low cost, producing clones. Either through licensing patents or technology acquisition, but without undertaking expensive R&D themselves, this allows manufacturers to copy the market leaders, benefiting from their earlier innovation, and to grow in domestic markets before competing on the world stage. Compaq's first PCs were IBM clones, using the same operating system but at a cheaper price and enabling the company to become one of the fastest growing in US history. In a different sector, since 1989 Molson Dry and Anheuser-Busch's Budweiser dry beer have together dominated the market for this particular product, whose manufacturing process was copied from the original Japanese Asashi and Sapporo products. Daewoo, also manufacturers of IBM clones, have grown a significant automotive presence based upon the use of previous generation General Motors' hardware such as engines, transmissions and substructures, whilst Samsung's initial growth was through producing low cost copies of Sharp microwave ovens. This has therefore been the common entry strategy for many manufacturers, particularly in the fast developing newly industrialized economies, and a base from where such companies as Compaq, Sharp and Samsung have developed and moved towards the more profitable defensive approach.

Lastly, outside the high technology product areas, there are a few companies who have been able to follow the *traditional* approach. In established markets where there is little call for change in the product and innovation has little role, manufacturers such as Barbour, Aga, Le Creuset and Mont Blanc are able to continue making the same products year on year. By a dictate of fashion, a number of niche markets for such brand name goods have developed where the constant consumer demand allows for profitable manufacture. This is however a group into which companies can rarely plan to move, being primarily subordinate on styling trends, customer preferences and in some cases seasonality.

Whichever of these four approaches are taken or combined is clearly influenced by the markets in which a company operates, its corporate objectives and business strategy. Which approach is followed therefore correspondingly effects the focus of the new product development strategy and how the product development activities are themselves subsequently undertaken. Manufacturers able to enter successfully and survive in the traditional group may only need occasionally to change a product's colour or packaging whilst those in the imitative category are regularly looking for cheaper suppliers for existing products and opportunities to acquire new products complementary to their facilities and their market. However, it is primarily in only those organizations following the offensive and defensive approaches that new product development in terms of the actual development of previously unavailable products is a major activity and is consequently an area which demands significant strategic attention.

For such manufacturers, new product strategies not only draw upon the influences of the other derivative strategies identified above, but also generate a number of additional second level strategies (Figure 1.4) specific to new product development, including dedicated R&D, design, manufacturing and marketing strategies. These may address the short, medium and long term needs and influences from a number of key contributory

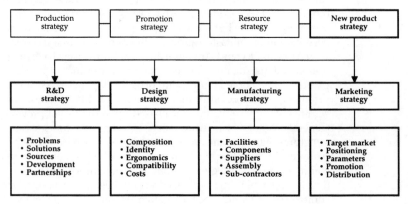

Figure 1.4 New product strategy

areas and collectively result in the development of products relevant to both the new product and hence the business strategies. Although inherently inter-linked at both the product and the organizational levels, each can be described separately.

R&D strategy

Particularly for those manufacturers following either offensive or defensive approaches to product development, the role of research and development is critical. In technology-dependent companies, ensuring that the research undertaken is relevant, practicable and appropriate to their individual needs is a major task and, to enable this to be achieved effectively, most successful organizations formulate and follow coherent R&D strategies. In large innovation-driven organizations such as 3M, Hewlett Packard, Philips and GE, the diverse range of technology-intensive activities demand clear focus, coordination and resourcing, whilst in smaller companies developing far fewer new products, the need to analyse, plan and control this core element of the development process is also crucial. Although the individual tasks undertaken by R&D personnel differ from one organization to another, the overall principles associated with the R&D strategies adopted are generically similar and can be seen to be influenced by five core issues:

- the key technological problems which need to be addressed in order to enable the new product to function as desired,
- the technology solutions that may be available to solve these problems,
- the range of sources of this technology from both within and outside the organization,
- the potential need to develop new solutions, and
- the partnership opportunities that could be utilized to help to achieve this.

Design strategy

While the R&D strategy typically addresses primarily technological issues, the design strategy is based on factors relating to how the appropriate technology is integrated within products to meet the needs of the marketplace. The design strategy effectively lays down the parameters which determine the nature of the product being developed, and therefore addresses not only how it will appear visually and be configured, but also how it may relate to the environment, the user and other products. Like the other second level strategies, there are elements which vary between different companies operating in different sectors, but the design strategy can also be seen to be influenced by five core generic issues:

- the intended composition of the product and how constituent components may be interfaced,
- the desired identity of the product, not only in terms of its shape and colour but also relating to any texture, pattern or corporate logo that may be applied to it,

- the specific ergonomic requirements that the product may wish to satisfy in order that it may be both comfortable and easy to use,
- the compatibility required between the product and industry standards or other products, and
- the typical cost constraints that apply to the product in relation to its components, their assembly and the anticipated retail price.

Manufacturing strategy

Both the R&D and design strategies examine how new products are to be created, but it is the manufacturing strategy which addresses how they are to be realized. Essentially assessing the options available for a new product's manufacture and assembly, manufacturing strategy enables the formulation of a plan for producing high quality products as efficiently as possible. Again largely specific to each company and their particular capabilities, manufacturing strategies can also be considered to be influenced by five core factors:

- the varied production facilities that are available to the organization,
- the typology and cost of components likely to be integrated within new products,
- the reliable and economic suppliers of these components,
- the options available for assembly of the products, and
- how sub-contractors may be used to either decrease cost, maintain a balanced production level or increase product quality.

Marketing strategy

Lastly, the marketing strategy frequently has a wider focus than the other derivative strategies, generally determining the context within which the product will be used and sold. Therefore, whereas the R&D, design and manufacturing strategies address the creation and realization of a new product, the marketing strategy primarily focuses upon its promotion and distribution. Whilst in some companies, undertaking pre-development market research is part of the development process, in many this is considered as a separate issue and does not itself form part of the marketing strategy. Thus although again variable between different organizations, the typical marketing strategy can be seen to be influenced by five core areas:

- identifying the target market, the customer, the existing price ranges and the expected features,
- determining the positioning of the new products within this market,
- defining what specific market, price and feature parameters should be addressed by the product,
- developing the advertising and promotion methods for the product and the associated packaging issues, and
- defining the appropriate distribution options and networks and identifying and liaising with retailers to help define pricing structures.

Product range

Lying at the heart of any manufacturing organization is the range of products that it manufactures. The manufacture and selling of the product range not only generates corporate income but, more significantly, is the *raison d'etre* of the company. It reflects both the historic and current areas of interest and sometimes, by indicating the areas in which a company is active, it can also be seen to indicate in what direction it may be moving.

Whilst some companies choose to manufacture a diverse range of products for many different markets, many others concentrate on niche specializations: Some large multinationals manufacture and sell thousands of different products and many companies prosper by concentrating on just a few. However, no matter at what point between these extremes a manufacturer may choose to operate, it is usual for each and every product to be appropriate to the company's current and, more significantly, future needs and resources. Therefore, if a housewares manufacturer has for instance traditionally produced products primarily composed of plastic mouldings and intends to continue doing so, adding the capability to manufacture additional products dependent on the use of, say, aluminium castings may well be inappropriate.

Although many of the world's manufacturing companies often produce a whole range of different products, some of which may initially appear to have little connection with one another, in the most successful organizations there is either one or more common factor between the products which provides synergy with corporate technological and organizational capabilities. These common factors are often termed the core competences and are the common elements which run through all the products.

Honda manufacture motorbikes, cars, vans, snowmobiles, tractors, lawnmowers, chain-saws, generators and outboard engines. Although this may appear to be a disparate list of products, they are all dependent on one critical area – transmissions and power-trains. All involve the transmission of power to, within or from an engine and this is an area of technical excellence within Honda, an area in which they can be considered to be at the forefront and hence an area upon which all their products are based. The core technology and knowledge associated with transmissions not only gives the organization the opportunity to develop the wide range of products but enables it to increase the added value by acting as both supplier and assembler.

Similarly Canon have their own core competences: they have management expertise in the effective use of development teams and achieving the highly efficient development processes found in many Japanese companies. They have marketing expertise relating to their brand and distribution networks and they have technological expertise in optics, electronics, imaging and precision mechanics. All of these core competences are evident in the products which they manufacture, ranging from cameras and copiers to laser-writers and fax machines, and when appropriately linked together with excellent market and user awareness, they all help to give Canon's products the all-important competitive edge over many of their rivals.

On a smaller scale, battery manufacturers Duracell grew their business steadily over a number of years and in the early 1980s were looking for opportunities to further increase sales. Initially conceived as a means for selling more products, the low cost matt black Durabeam torch was hugely successful, increasing turnover and taking a major share of the torch market and making a significant contribution to Duracell's profits. Although a new venture for the company into a field in which it had not previously been active, this move was also built upon its core competence of battery manufacture, to which the new products added value.

Therefore, when determining strategies for new product development, it is common for manufacturers to identify their existing and envisaged core competences and ensure that they match the proposed new products. Whilst some companies are based around *core technologies* such as gas analysis, some around *core capabilities* such as low cost plastics manufacture and others around *core assets* such as distribution networks, most successful organizations ensure that both their current and future product ranges complement these competences and thereby enable the company concerned to further progress and exploit their areas of expertise.

Depending upon the overall business strategy, particular market characteristics, technological developments and the company's product range, there are a number of differing opportunities available to manufacturers for the development of new products. The accompanying case history of the Rover 600 illustrates a new product strategy founded upon the joint development of a new vehicle based on an existing product, however this is only one of many approaches. Given the range of alternatives of developing a totally new invention, producing an incrementally improved version of an existing product, copying an existing design, extending or focusing a product range and doing these independently, in partnerships or via licence agreements, there are numerous permutations possible.

HP OmniShare

Hewlett Packard is an international US-based manufacturer of measurement and computation products and systems. The company's products and services are used in industry, business, engineering, science, medicine and education in over 100 countries. It employs almost 100,000 people and in 1993 had a turnover of over $20 billion.

In 1992 Hewlett Packard and US telecommunications company AT&T started working together on a new range of products. Both organizations had their own strengths in communication and computer technology, and as these areas had gradually moved closer together over the previous decade, it became apparent to both organizations that as a partnership they could develop a totally new type of product.

Within the communications market, the success of the original facsimile machine in 1986 as a means of quickly transferring letters, memos or drawings had driven the development of a number of other derivative products such as plain paper and colour fax. In addition the growth of digital networks enabling multi-site telephone calls and video-conferencing had changed the way in which many organizations and people within them communicate. In computing, the massive expansion of the use of PCs throughout business and education had provided the majority of professionals direct or indirect access to information technology whilst the associated development of modems and electronic mail had begun to bring the two product sectors closer and closer together.

There was however perceived to be a gap in the market for a product which would allow people in two locations to share graphics, text and annotations while simultaneously speaking to each other: a product which would allow both data and voice to be transmitted simultaneously, ideally across a standard telephone line. This would enable users to bring together all of their existing systems and collaborate on work using faxes, PCs and video-conferencing.

AT&T had already developed 'Voice Span' technology which allowed simultaneous voice and data communications over a single, standard telephone line and offered significant advantages over other systems which required either expensive ISDN lines or alternating voice and data transmission. By integrating this technology within the development of a HP product, it was decided that the desired device could be realistically manufactured and marketed to a wide range of users. Hewlett Packard therefore assembled an array of technology companies to develop what became the HP OmniShare conferencer: Logitech for its electronic pen technology, Hitachi for its liquid crystal display (LCD) expertise and Travelling Software Inc. for its communications software.

Over the following two years these companies developed a product which both of the primary partners felt would have immediate use in environments where time and convenience were highly valued. It enabled users to load documents either from a PC or via a standard fax machine or modem into a notebook-sized hand-held tablet where an image of the document was produced. Then, by connecting this to another via a standard phone line, two or more users could annotate the documents, writing or drawing on the tablet using an electronic pen, seeing each other's comments or sketches in real time whilst simultaneously talking to each other. In addition the product enabled users to also flip through up to 500 pages of information, rotate graphics or zoom-in on specific details and print out the documents either through a standard printer or fax machine. It thereby helped to achieve a faster and more effective discussion and agreement between parties and potentially reduced costs by avoiding the need to either meet in person or use courier services.

By forming strategic alliances with other companies who had the necessary capabilities to enable the envisaged product to function effectively, Hewlett Packard were able to enter the facsimile market, creating a new sector which they and their partners could dominate. None of the five organizations individually had the technology or knowledge to develop such a product alone, but by working together and each making their own contribution they were collectively able to be part of the OmniShare and gain a strong foothold in a market which in 1994 was worth over $10 billion worldwide. As with the Rover 600 discussed in the accompanying case study, this product was developed following new product strategies which were each appropriate to the organizations concerned at the time, fulfilling customer-driven market demands, meeting each company's requirement for new product and associated revenue and supporting their overall business strategies.

Continual development

Once a company launches a successful new product, no matter how well protected it is by international patents or how well controlled are the distribution channels, if it is a successful product, all too often someone, somewhere, will copy it. Illegal direct copies are made to capitalize on a strong brand name – replicas of products such as Cartier watches, Ray Ban sunglasses and Nike sports shoes are routinely manufactured in countries where poor regulation allows it, whilst in areas where legislation is more developed and enforceable, many companies manufacture almost identical products purely to benefit from the short-term opportunity before patent protection can be imposed through the courts.

The most common route for most manufacturers operating in developed markets is the imitation of a new product by competitors following a defensive strategy. As discussed earlier, this popular approach to product development may sometimes involve a technologically more or less identical product, repackaged or restyled in some manner or, alternatively, an incrementally improved product incorporating a new feature. In such cases, there is no legal means of preventing what is effectively competition and so, to protect their market share, manufacturers are forced to react and develop their own improved models. In order to maintain a position as the innovator in a field, companies therefore have to develop a second or third generation product, sometimes even before the first one is launched. This frequently results in a number of companies developing products which systematically 'leap frog' each other either technically or visually: mobile phone manufacturers are constantly launching new products with improved reception, additional features and restyled casings and interfaces purely as a means of ensuring that they have a product available which matches customer requirements. Only through a continuous series of incremental improvements to an original product can manufacturers capitalize on the innovation, ensure that the market share is protected and maintain a steady income from the product to repay the original investment and support future development. Although this occurs in all areas of manufacturing from cars and computers to pet food, perhaps the most widely recognized examples are found in consumer electronics of which the most popular is the Sony Walkman.

Sony Walkman

As one of the leading innovators in consumer electronics, Sony first introduced the Walkman in 1979. Although by today's standards the first model was large, bulky and, in terms of sound quality and features, relatively basic, at the time it was a significant innovative leap which created and exploited a whole new market. For the first time it gave consumers a genuinely portable music system which was also personal and, to a certain extent, private. However, technologically it contained nothing new, being effectively a repacking of existing components and was therefore difficult to protect. As worldwide sales grew rapidly, Sony's competitors such as Aiwa, Panasonic and Toshiba all produced and launched their own versions to also benefit from the growing market. In order to maintain their market share and leading position in the field, Sony therefore had continually to develop and launch improved products. Only by doing this would they be able to retain their lead, capitalize on their innovation and generate a significant contribution to their business turnover.

Table 1.2   Walkman innovation 1979–1988

Feature	Company	Date	Imitated
Walkman	Sony	1979	Yes
Mini headphones	Sony	1979	Yes
AM/FM stereo radio	Sony	1980	Yes
Stereo recording	Sony/Aiwa	1980–81	Yes
FM tuner cassette	Toshiba	1980–81	No
Auto-reverse	KLH SOLO	1981–82	Yes
FM headphone radio	Sony	1981–82	Yes
Downsized unit	Sony	1982	Yes
Dolby	Sony/Aiwa	1982	Yes
Direct drive	Sony	1982	No
Cassette-sized unit	Sony	1983	Yes
Shortwave tuner	Sony	1983	No
Remote control	Aiwa	1983	Yes
Detachable speakers	Aiwa	1983	Yes
Water resistance	Sony	1983–4	No
Graphic equalizer	Sony	1985	Yes
Rechargeable	Sony	1985	Yes
Solar-powered	Sony	1986	No
Radio presets	Panasonic	1986	Yes
Dual cassettes	Sony	1986	No
TV audio band	Sony	1986–87	No
Digital tuning	Panasonic	1986–87	Yes
Child's model	Sony	1987	Yes
Enhanced bass	Sony	1987–88	Yes
Voice activated	Toshiba	1988	No

Source: S.W. Sanderson and V. Uzumeri (1990) *Strategies for New Product Development and Renewal: Design-Based Incrementalism*. Arthur D. Little.

Over the next ten years there were many significant improvements made to the original product, most of which were quickly imitated (Table 1.2). Some of these were introduced by Sony themselves and some by their competitors. However it was Sony who were predominant in this continuous innovation and who consequently continually led the field: Sony were the first to introduce an FM radio feature in 1980, the first to reduce significantly the product's size in 1982, the first to produce a 'sports' version in 1983, the first to launch rechargeable models in 1985 and with the 'my first Sony' range, the first to manufacture a child's version in 1987. These developments, orientated towards clearly identified groups of prospective purchasers, have continually increased the number of models manufactured by Sony more than their competition and, in doing so, have enabled the company to protect their market share, to nurture the market and ensure that nearly twenty years after initial development, the Walkman continues to be a profitable product and has become synonymous with the whole personal stereo market.

Although this example demonstrates one extreme, the basic principle of achieving continuous development to maintain market share and ensure continued profitability applies across the vast majority of product sectors. Wherever a manufacturer faces competition, continually developing new and improved products is critical and even where competitors do not immediately provide a significant threat, providing consumers with more efficient, better made and lower cost products that meet their expectations is one of the key means of increasing market presence, recognition, sales and therefore income.

Chapter summary

This chapter has provided an overview of some of the many influences on business and new product strategy. It has discussed some of the internal and external influences on an organization's business strategy, identified the key derivative strategies and, focusing on the new product strategy, has examined one in more detail. The alternative strategic approaches to new product development have been identified and the various R&D, design, manufacturing and marketing strategies associated with product development have been described. Through the use of a number of pertinent examples, building upon core capabilities to develop a coherent product range and the importance of continually developing new products have both been illustrated. The key issues covered can be summarized as:

- Organizations develop a business strategy to meet their corporate objectives which are frequently encapsulated within a mission statement or strategic vision.
- The business strategy is influenced by the organization's internal strengths and weaknesses and external threats and opportunities.
- From the business strategy can be derived individual strategies addressing production, promotion, resources and new products.

- The alternative approaches available for new product development can generically be identified as offensive, defensive, imitative and traditional.
- Subordinate to the new product strategy are the four inter-related R&D, manufacturing, design and marketing strategies.
- Successful manufacturers' product ranges are built upon and around either their own or partners' core technological, organizational and intellectual competences.
- To increase market share and maintain an established lead, the continual development of more efficient, economical and user orientated new products is now a necessity.

References

Ansoff, H.I. (1987) *Corporate Strategy.* Penguin.

Freeman, C. (1982) *The Economics of Industrial Innovation.* 2nd edition, Francis Pinter, London.

Kay, J.A. (1993) *Foundations of Corporate Success: How Business Strategies Add Value.* Oxford University Press.

McGrath, M.E. (1995) *Product Strategy for High Technology Companies.* Irwin.

Morita, A. (1987) *Made in Japan.* HarperCollins.

Pascale, R.T. and Athos, A.G. (1981) *The Art of Japanese Management.* Penguin.

Schnaars, S.P. (1994) *Managing Imitation Strategies: How Late Entrants Seize Markets from Pioneers.* Free Press.

Tasker, P. (1987) *Inside Japan: Wealth, Work and Power on the New Japanese Empire.* Penguin.

Case study 1: Rover 600

The Rover Group is Britain's largest motor manufacturer, producing approximately half a million vehicles a year. Now owned by BMW, the group designs, manufactures and markets small, medium and executive cars and specialist four-wheel drive vehicles. These products are sold in more than 100 countries and generate an annual sales revenue in excess of £4000 million. In Europe, their main competitors include multinationals such as Ford, GM and VW-Audi, specialist manufacturers such as Saab, Mercedes and Alfa-Romeo and, increasingly more significant, Japanese companies such as Toyota, Nissan and Honda.

Although one of a number of independent UK manufacturers from the beginning of the century, following nationalization in the 1960s, product quality dropped and market share correspondingly declined. As British Leyland, in 1979 the company began a partnership with Honda based on the joint development of mutually beneficial products. Since then a range of products including the Rover 200, 400 and 800 Series have been designed with Honda and the two companies have developed their UK manufacturing facilities in parallel.

Following privatization in 1988, Rover Group identified the upper medium premium sector of the market as one area for which a new vehicle should be developed. Directly competing with cars such as the BMW 3 Series and Audi 80, the new product would fill a gap in the product range and help to position Rover as a specialist manufacturer of high-quality vehicles. Jointly developed with Honda, the Rover 600 was launched in April 1993 and sold over 50,000 units in its first twelve months of production. Widely praised as one of the best British cars to have been developed in recent years, the car won several accolades including a 1994 British Design Council Award.

This case study describes the development of the Rover 600, focusing in particular on the strategic decisions involved. Following a brief history of the company, it gives an overview of the relationship between Rover and Honda and discusses the key issues associated with the development of the vehicle. It identifies the key strategic aims of the project and describes how each of the subsequent marketing, design and manufacturing objectives were met.

Background

The Rover Group is now what remains of a number of British independent manufacturers such as Triumph, Austin, Morris, Riley, Standard, Wolseley and Alvis who in the late 1960s were all brought together under the nationalized umbrella organization of the British Leyland Motor Corporation (Figure C1.1). This move was initiated primarily to create a British volume production capability able to compete with the likes of Ford, GM and the major European and Japanese manufacturers. However, over the subsequent years this company has moved from being a large volume

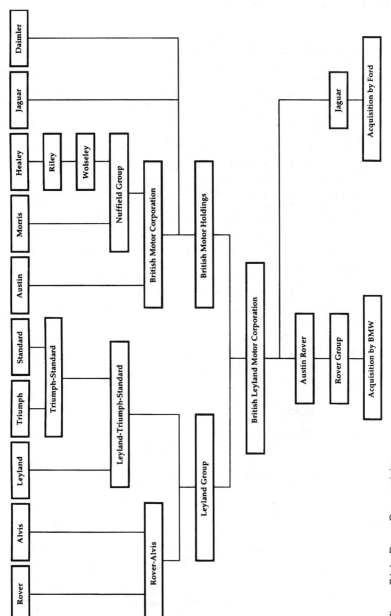

Figure C1.1 Rover Group origins

manufacturer with a diverse range of products supporting most of the original marques, firstly to Austin Rover in the early 1980s and then to the Rover Group in the 1990s with a single coherent product range.

The Rover name itself can be traced back to the beginning of the century when the Coventry-based Rover Cycle Company first started manufacturing cars such as the 1905 Rover 8 and the 1907 Rover 20. Like the other British vehicle manufacturers of the time, Rover grew steadily and throughout the 1930s and 1940s developed into a leading producer of quality large cars such as the Rover 14 and 16. During the 1950s and early 1960s, the Rover P4 and P5 became some of Britain's most successful luxury vehicles, competing with the likes of Jaguar and Daimler. In the late 1960s the Rover 2000 was the first car to be orientated specifically at the executive market and in 1976 the SD1 continued the Rover tradition, filling a gap in the British Leyland product range between Austin-Morris and Jaguar vehicles.

However as standards of design and manufacture dropped in the Austin-Morris division of British Leyland, resulting in a range of uninspiring products such as the Morris Marina, Austin Princess and a subsequent overall decline in market share, the Jaguar-Rover-Triumph division of the organization looked for an external partner and in 1979 began working with Japanese manufacturer Honda who wished to increase their presence in the European market. Under this relationship a number of vehicles were to be developed sharing technology, components and, where appropriate, platforms. These would be marketed by both Honda and British Leyland, allowing the one vehicle to be sold under two brands and thereby hopefully achieving higher overall sales. The first product of this collaborative relationship was the development of a modified Honda Ballade which was launched in 1981 as the Triumph Acclaim. During the 1980s the relative success of this model led to further joint development of products bearing the more prestigious Rover name such as the 1984 Rover 200 and the 1986 Rover 800 Series.

New products

As part of the UK government's ongoing privatization programme, in August 1988 the company was sold to British Aerospace who were then keen to develop their business into sectors outside their traditional core aerospace and defence manufacturing. It was clear that, although Rover was at the time manufacturing 40 per cent of cars being built in Britain, despite the recent joint ventures with Honda, the company was neither producing nor selling at levels which allowed it to compete on cost with other major volume manufacturers such as Ford, GM, Toyota, Nissan and Peugeot-Citroen. Given a growing total over-capacity of car production within Europe, it was unlikely that Rover would be able to increase production significantly and consequently, to survive in this ever increasingly competitive market, it had to reposition itself as a specialist manufacturer. In order to achieve this, a decision was taken to focus upon the Rover name, its premium marque, and concentrate on the production of vehicles appropriate to this level. Working ever more closely with Honda, Rover Group would develop a new range of prestige products and re-establish a market position around the Rover name, competing not only with the upper range Ford, GM and Toyota vehicles but also with premium marques such as BMW, Mercedes, Audi.

The partnership that existed with Honda was based upon the joint development of mutually beneficial products. Whilst the two companies would cooperate on such cars as the Rover 800/Honda Legend, both were free to pursue independently other products under their own resources. For Rover this primarily involved the small car Metro and Mini markets and the successful 4 × 4 sector comprising the Land Rover, Range Rover and the recently introduced Discovery, whilst Honda continued to develop the Civic, NSX sports-car and Prelude. Therefore at the time of the sale to British Aerospace, the Rover Group's car product range (Figure C1.2) comprised the old but still successful 1959 Mini, the reasonably well performing 1980 Metro, the 1983 Maestro and 1984 Montego for which there was a sufficient demand to maintain production until the end of 1994, and the 1984 Rover 200 and 1986 Rover 800, both of which had been developed with Honda, with whom Rover by now had a 20 per cent equity cross shareholding. The continued partnership was therefore considered to offer a sound basis upon which to develop some of Rover's new vehicles to expand and replace some of this range.

The Rover 800 series gave the company a presence in the executive market, whilst the new Rover 200 and derived 400 series, sharing common platforms with the latest Honda Concerto, were both to be manufactured in Longbridge and launched in October 1989 and March 1990 respectively to compete with mainstream products in the lower medium vehicle market. This left a gap in the product range for an upper medium premium product to compete directly with cars such as the BMW 3 series and Audi 80. While the Montego remained a good competitor for the basic Ford Sierra and Vauxhall Cavalier, carrying the Austin marque it did not fit in with the positioning aspirations for the Rover brand and the development of this vehicle was hence inappropriate. So, if Rover were to develop a new car for this market, an early decision therefore had to be made whether to do it either independently or alternatively in partnership with Honda. A major influence upon this decision was that the planned production of 50,000 cars per annum was, by car industry standards, relatively low and therefore the new vehicle would have to return a profit when sold at these volumes. Therefore the new product objective became to develop a new premium upper medium product that could sell profitably in low volumes and be incremental in sales to the existing and planned range.

At the end of the 1980s Rover were assembling the Concerto and Legend for Honda to sell within Europe and also supporting Honda in setting up a manufacturing facility in Swindon to provide power units for both Honda and Rover products. In 1989, Honda saw an opportunity to develop this site into vehicle assembly for the European market using a version of the existing upper medium Ascott Innova vehicle, at the time being manufactured in

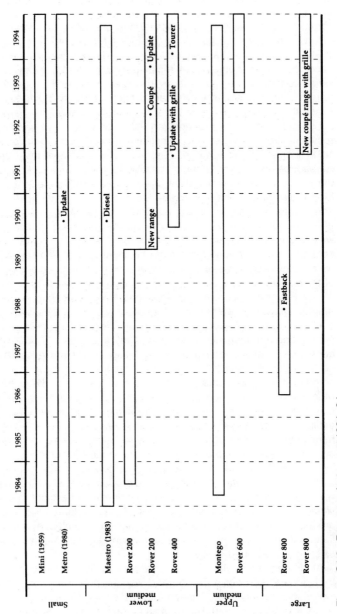

Figure C1.2 Rover product range 1984–94

Japan. This car, the new Accord, would share the same platform as the Japanese model but, to help satisfy the 80 per cent local content requirement for vehicles assembled in Europe, would source engines from the new Swindon plant and other components from across the region. In developing this European supplier base, Honda recognized Rover to be the best supplier of pressed steel body panels and consequently Rover's body pressing facility, also located in Swindon, won the contract to supply the 'body in white' for the Accord. Rover saw that this would provide an opportunity to short circuit the development programme for the planned upper medium vehicle and, since a high percentage of components for such a product were already scheduled to be manufactured in the UK either by Honda or Rover themselves, it was felt opportune to initiate the development of a new car, the Rover 600, sharing any appropriate parts and production facilities with the Accord. Discussions about the development of such a vehicle were started in 1989 and a subsequent development agreement between the two companies was signed in April 1990.

This strategy of jointly developing a car to meet Rover's objective would be beneficial to the company in several ways. It would primarily enable them to share the development costs with Honda and, because the product would be based on an existing design, it could be developed in a far shorter timescale than the traditional five years. It would not draw excessively upon the company's engineering resources which were then committed to developing a new Range Rover, a new MG sports car and new 200 and 400 models. It would provide a means for Rover to add value to body panels which they would be making anyway, and, because the overall capital costs for the new car were therefore relatively low, it would also free sufficient funds to be invested in the consolidation of manufacturing facilities, particularly the rebuilding of Cowley, which were necessary to achieve a leaner, more efficient manufacturing base. From Honda's perspective, the joint development would both strengthen the partnership and reduce the cost of many of their components. In particular it would halve the direct costs of tooling their new engine plant and double its projected overall output volume, enabling the investment to be spread across more units, and thereby reducing the piece cost of each engine.

However, to achieve successfully the overall company objective by following this strategy, Rover needed to identify the specific requirements for the product in terms of the key areas involved. Although there was no significant R&D objective as the product was to be based on an existing platform and incorporate largely existing technology, there were nevertheless key aims for for marketing, design and manufacture (Figure C1.3). In these three areas, the primary objectives would be:

- **From the marketing perspective:** to position the 600 as a high quality British product which was both prestigious and accessible.
- **From the design perspective:** to differentiate the 600 from the Honda Accord and transform it into a Rover whilst using as many common components as possible.

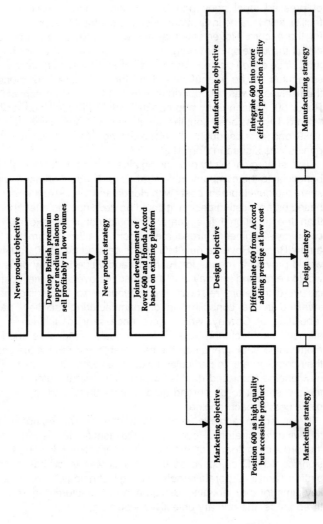

Figure C1.3 Rover 600 new product development strategy and derivative objectives

● **From the manufacturing perspective:** to integrate it into a more efficient production facility at Cowley without causing major disruption to existing vehicle production.

To achieve each of these individual objectives, three mutually dependent strategies were subsequently developed.

Marketing

In developing the marketing strategy for the 600, not only did Rover have to clearly identify the market sector in which the product was to compete and ascertain the relative strengths and weaknesses of both the existing and envisaged competition, but also determine the principal characteristics and expectations of the target customer base. In the upper medium sub-class of cars, the true retail buyer is a rarity, generally being either relatively wealthy or a retiring executive. However in the larger fleet car market, which would provide 80 per cent of the projected sales, there were several key factors identified as commonly governing product selection. Perhaps the most influential of these was style and car and driver imagery and, as one of the key targets for the 600 were business professionals who would previously have not considered the Rover marque as being appropriate to the image they would like to project, positioning the product successfully here was therefore critical. Hence to both retain existing Rover users and attract new customers away from the competition it was these aspects of the product which had to be carefully addressed in order to establish the 600 as a distinctive British product with all the necessary executive values.

In this sector the definitive benchmark at the time was the Mercedes 190. It benefited from the highly dependable, well engineered reputation of all Mercedes products and at around £20,000 offered customers Mercedes build quality at an entry level price. Competing in the same class, the BMW 3 series, Audi 80, Saab 900 and Alfa Romeo 155 all had established reputations and recognized driver imagery whilst new entrants from Japan such as the Mazda Xedos 6 were also building on their proven reliability and quality standards to target this lucrative segment. In addition, some of the larger volume manufacturers were developing several medium sized coupés such as the GM Calibra and Ford Probe to also compete in this price area. Thus with such rival products, positioning the Rover 600 to succeed in this market was certainly far from straightforward for the company.

At the time of the development of the 600, Rover still had a public image that was largely based upon its recent history. Together with low corporate awareness throughout Europe and a recent withdrawal from the US market, a lingering reputation for industrial disputes and low quality from the British Leyland era continued to hinder the company and its products. Whilst the 1989 200, 1990 400 and 1991 800 series were laying the foundations for new Rover products, the company wanted the 600 to be a fundamental change: a high quality car that would alter opinions and be seen as a new type of

Rover product thereby improving the overall image of all the company's products as well as Rover as a manufacturer. To achieve this marketing personnel therefore worked closely with the design team in identifying the key details which would add the necessary style to engender the product with the desired appeal and in selecting the appropriate colour/trim combinations to further enhance this image.

In addition to overall style and car/driver image, the other major factor in the purchase decision for the business market is cost of ownership. Whichever products are selected for fleet markets, discounted retail price, anticipated depreciation and maintenance costs are all heavily influential and Rover therefore wanted the 600 to score highly in all three. However, whilst the Honda reputation for reliability and quality would guarantee low maintenance cost, achieving a comparatively low purchase price would require more effort for, although the prestige image and design were intended to be more representative of a £25,000 car, Rover wanted to price the entry level model at only £15,000, both undercutting the established specialist BMW and Audi competition and offering higher quality and greater driver appeal than top of the range Cavaliers and Mondeos.

The means of achieving this, adopted from the established specialist prestige car manufacturers, was to reduce the specification of the base models, a measure which was known not to be a major factor in fleet car purchase decisions. Rather than incorporating most of the options in the entry level £15,000 vehicle – as the large volume manufacturers were accustomed to doing to increase perceived value – it was decided that such extras as ABS, alloy wheels, leather upholstery and electric rear windows would only be included in more expensive £17,000, £18,000 and £20,000 models. Working closely with manufacturing to identify these features and determine the key model differentiates, following this strategy not only enabled the production cost of the base model to be reduced to the required levels but also ensured that the pricing structure across the whole range would be more profitable.

To support this definition of specification/cost ratios and the positioning of the product, attention was also paid to the values by which the car would be promoted. Given the market and the particular competitive advantages that Rover had built up, it was decided that these would be very high quality in conjunction with accessibility. The relationship with Honda had helped to establish the reputation for reliability and its quality image could be built upon in advertisements by emphasizing features such as the car's pedigree and its very low noise levels. In addition, by ensuring that the product's good value for money was simultaneously communicated to prospective customers, it was envisaged that they would also feel that the 600 was an attainable product. This would enable the 600 to be launched successfully as a serious competitor in this section of the market and, through utilizing the car's qualities and raising the company's reputation, help both it and future products such as the 1995 400 series to perform well in sales.

Thus, by concentrating upon these three core factors of prestige image, cost of ownership and promotion values, in partnership with the rest of the project team, marketing personnel were able to develop an overall package which would appropriately address the prescribed objectives and accurately position the car within the chosen market sector.

Design

A key advantage of following the joint development strategy was minimizing the cost of the new car in terms of investment required for tooling of parts. By maintaining as many common components as possible between the Accord and the 600, the anticipated expenditure was shared between the two companies. However, whilst adopting this approach, there was the need to differentiate the two vehicles and, from Rover's perspective, to add the necessary styling features to position the 600 as a distinctive, prestigious and aspirational product. Whereas in the past, the Rover models which had arisen from the partnership had mainly been re-badged versions of Honda vehicles, with this project it was felt that a more recognizable differentiation was necessary. In achieving this, the major problem which faced the Rover design team was that the body structure and dynamics of the two vehicles were to remain identical – the same transmission, electronics and suspension were all to be incorporated within the same body. The only components which were eligible for redesign were therefore those which formed either the exterior or interior surfaces of the product, where modification would not affect assembly (Figure C1.4). The designers were hence unable to change anything which would alter any of the key datum points such as wheelbase, position of windscreen, doors, steering wheel, etc., as these were all fixed.

Figure C1.4 Rover 600 series cut-away. Reproduced by kind permission of Rover Group Limited

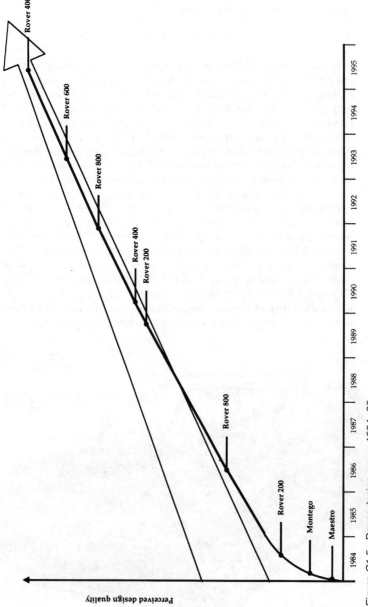

Figure C1.5 Rover design arrow 1984–95

For several years there had been a strong movement within Rover towards improving both the design and build quality of their cars and, as an internal means of communicating progress, the designers had adopted a design arrow (Figure C1.5) to map both existing vehicles and those still in development. This enabled the perceived levels of design quality and image for future projects to be effectively related to current models and allowed design targets in terms of style and prestige to be identified. Whereas the Maestro and Montego were well below the desired range, the 1984 200 and the 1986 800 were closer and the 1989 200 and 1990 400 were just inside. The 1991 800 would be within the planned standard, but with the 600 they wanted to be right on target, defining a modern Rover vehicle, and the company, as a high quality specialist manufacturer.

The main means by which cars are visually differentiated from one another are the overall body form, size and key design details, particularly at the front and rear of the vehicles. Because of the necessary commonality, in this case there was no possibility of changing the overall form or size and consequently the higher level of design style and quality would have to be achieved by altering these other details. Therefore, to identify which were appropriate, a design audit of all potential components was undertaken and each part was approached and evaluated separately to ascertain whether a redesign would achieve the desired effect, meeting the design objective but without adding unnecessary or unjustifiable cost. This identified only a

Figure C1.6 Rover 600 series. Reproduced by kind permission of Rover Group Limited

handful of components as being available for redesign, so successfully modifying these became the key task for the designers. Whatever choices were taken had to be right, for in this market there would be little opportunity for a second attempt.

The design team needed to create a visual corporate identity not just for the 600 but also for future Rover cars (Figure C1.6). In doing this they could either adopt references from existing or earlier Rover vehicles which were felt to be appropriate or alternatively introduce new features. However, because of the many changes which had taken place within the company and its products over the previous decade, established design cues that were considered suitable were relatively few in number.

Externally, the identified areas available for redesign were concentrated on the front (Figure C1.7) and rear (Figure C1.8). Whereas the 1989 200/400 had similar bonnet/headlamp/grille arrangements as both the 1986 800 and the earlier Montego, the revised 1991 800 was to incorporate a new radiator grille, similar in design to those found on some of the company's earlier cars of the 1940s and 1950s such as the Rover P4 and P5. It drew heavily on Rover's heritage and was a feature which the company wished to incorporate elsewhere in its product range and was consequently also to be progressively introduced to revised versions of the 200 and 400 in 1992 and 1993. Maintaining this feature in the 600 would therefore provide a visual link between all the new cars. However, since the 600 was to be the clear definition of a new Rover, it was decided to update the existing grille design,

Figure C1.7   Rover 620ti. Reproduced by kind permission of Rover Group Limited

Figure C1.8 Rover 620ti. Reproduced by kind permission of Rover Group Limited

adding a little more chrome and smoothing its corners. At the same time the opportunity was taken to integrate single piece front lighting units giving greater coherence than the separate headlamp and indicator units used on existing vehicles. Together with a more rounded front bumper, these two features necessitated only minor modification to the bonnet and front wing but successfully established a new image which, although different, was identifiable as a new Rover and could also be incorporated into major new vehicle developments such as the 1995 400 series.

At the rear of the vehicle there were no existing design features that were felt to be appropriate. At the time, there was little consistency across the rest of the product range in either shape of trunk or lighting unit and so the opportunity was taken to design a new rear which could also be used to influence future products. To echo the prestige styling, a chrome surround, similar in proportion and visual weight to the front grille, was also incorporated around the rear number plate recessed within the trunk. In sympathy with the use of chrome around the windows of the car, this ensured that the same imagery was continued around the vehicle and, together with a smoother rear bumper and new rear lighting units which were more rounded than existing products, helped to maintain the prestigious, high quality appearance.

Internally, two existing Rover design cues were felt to be worthy of adoption. The use of wooden inlay within the facia and doors was traditional to all Rover products and, although adding complexity to manufacture, was again incorporated. In addition, the corporate use of stainless steel tread-plates which had been used across the product range for the past thirty years was emphasized as a Rover hallmark. However, as it is the exterior of a car which primarily gives it its identity, besides the use of dedicated Rover fabrics, the majority of internal components such as seats, carpets and lights remained common with the Honda.

Thus by redesigning just these few key external components and incorporating existing Rover details inside, the designers were able to successfully change the overall style and image of the vehicle at relatively little cost. The majority of secondary and all primary parts remained identical to the Accord but, nevertheless, the perception given was that the 600 was a different, more refined product which could therefore be marketed at a higher level.

Manufacturing

For manufacturing, the integration of the new 600 series into the plant at Cowley was going to be a major task. There had initially been three sites at this location, all separated by major roads and manufacturing three different vehicles: pressings and bodies were all being produced at the Cowley body plant, the Maestro and Montego were being assembled at Cowley South and Rover 800 at Cowley North. It was clear that not only was this far too large a facility for the envisaged future volume of production but the logistics of operating it were also, to say the least, complex. Bodies which were assembled on one site had to be transported to another for painting and matching up with the power and transmission systems, interior components, windscreens and lights. Given the need to achieve a lean production facility to reduce production costs, and a commitment made as part of the sale to British Aerospace to balance overall capacity, the three sites had therefore to be consolidated into one.

Although the Maestro and Montego were by now ageing models, they were still selling reasonably, well above expectations, and it was therefore still viable for the company to maintain production. Consequently not only would the 600 most likely have to be produced on the same line as the 800 series, but the Maestro and Montego also had to be integrated into the same facility. Although a new version of the 800 series was scheduled to be launched at the end of 1991, at this time no changes to the design of any of the existing models were feasible and so, to minimize complexity of the production facility, it was going to be vital to make the manufacture of the 600 series as simple as possible. However, whilst it would be a more advanced car than the 800, having improved build quality and, because of its Honda background, was designed for lean manufacture, further improvements would also be necessary.

The Rover 800 was typical of the European build philosophy. Twenty different models were available in eleven different colours and features such as air-bags, anti-lock braking systems and sports seats were all available as optional extras. This gave the customer a wide range of possible combinations to choose from and, it was argued that, by enabling the customer's specific wishes to be met, it thereby increased the chances of individual purchases. However, for the production facility, this customer choice resulted in the possibility of either customized manufacture or, to ensure that the full range was always available, it meant that over 1500 different versions of the car were coming off the line to stock. Each car was unique and, as more labour was involved in a high specification model than in the basic car, it had also been traditional to space out and mix up production in order to balance the overall production system. Whilst Ford, GM, VW and many other high volume manufacturers adopted the same approach, if the production of the Rover 600 was to be as simple as realistically possible, this manufacturing option was not available and a more appropriate solution would be required.

In their Swindon plant Honda were planning to return to a batch build philosophy where groups of a minimum of thirty identical cars were made together. This was related to Honda's need to control the variables in producing a new factory, new suppliers, a new design in a new country with a new work force. Because of the advantages that such a system would offer and the necessarily close interface between the two facilities, Rover also chose to adopt the same approach for the 600 at Cowley. However, although it would minimize variation within the production facility, there was a problem with this option. If the same level of customer choice was offered, it could be months between production of the same models and this would lead to either long delivery periods or the need to build up an enormous stock of vehicles. Neither were acceptable and consequently, in order to make the system work, Rover had to reduce significantly the number of options available. Although commercially this was disadvantageous because a customer could not, for example, have a red car with leather seats, sunroof, electric windows and central door locking but no air conditioning, alloy wheels, air bag or CD player, by offering a smaller range of the most likely combinations, the benefits in manufacturing terms would be considerable.

It was therefore decided initially to produce only thirty different combinations of vehicle comprising six different models available in only five colour/fabric combinations, using only three different engines with options such as air-bag and anti-lock brakes fitted as standard on some models and unavailable on others. This restricted but carefully selected range would sufficiently simplify production, enabling labour costs to be kept down and hopefully not affect the product's commercial competitiveness. An additional benefit gained from this approach concerned the ordering of parts: although most were to be sourced from Europe, some key components would still have to come from Japan and, to allow for packaging and procurement, the system adopted demanded that these were ordered five months before build. Because Honda's build philosophy depends on the assembly of a kit of parts dedicated to each vehicle at source, the lead times involved are relatively long and once an order has been placed for committed production there is no way of changing it. Hence having a large range of model/option combinations would have resulted in major stock problems if demand patterns changed and keeping to this restricted range decreased the possibility of such an occurrence.

Therefore, by minimizing the production variables and adopting the batch build philosophy, Rover were able to ensure that the integration of the 600 into the consolidated production facility at Cowley was as smooth as possible, causing minimal disruption to existing lines and laying the foundation for more efficient manufacture throughout the company in the future.

Launch

The Rover 600 series (Figure C1.9) was launched in April 1993, only three years after the signing of the joint development agreement with Honda. It was received with high critical acclaim, being described as 'the most successful creation since the Honda partnership began' and 'despite its Japanese roots, being the closest thing to a British BMW so far conceived'. The decisions taken regarding production techniques, design details and product range paid off and by the end of 1994 85,000 vehicles had been produced. Of these 38,000 were sold in the UK, whilst in Europe, sales increased to 21,500 p.a., accounting for nearly 40 per cent of total production. Outselling the Honda Accord by a ratio of 5:1, the 600 thus helped Rover to once again become regarded as a quality manufacturer of prestige vehicles.

Figure C1.9 Rover 620ti. Reproduced by kind permission of Rover Group Limited

Continuous development

Planning the product range for launch was however only the first part of what became an ongoing development programme. Because of the relatively low European content at launch, the company were on the receiving end of an increasing yen/sterling exchange rate and were buying in a number of high value parts such as the power train, consequently the profit margins on every car would be low and so other means of generating more profit were looked for. Originally it had been agreed that for the 600, Rover would annually source 50,000 Honda-built engines from the new plant in Swindon. However, if, in addition to continuing to use all these, Rover could also incorporate some of their own engines, used on other Rover cars, two distinct benefits would be obtained. First, it would increase the product range and sales volume and, although it would add complexity to the manufacturing process, if these engines were used in otherwise identical models to the original six, the impact would be minimal. Second, if more cars could be sold, the overall volumes would increase and the mean manufacturing costs could be brought down.

In December 1990, over two years before initial product launch, two key opportunities were identified: having a diesel-powered model was strategically important as it provided a real opportunity for incremental volume and profit. Rover therefore saw an opportunity to develop a new diesel engine, the L series, which would be introduced in the 620 SDi/SLDi in 1995, could also be used in other Rover products and could also be supplied to Honda for the Accord. In addition a performance model boosting the range and car image would offer further increased sales in Europe, especially Italy. Therefore the decision was taken to introduce the 620ti in 1994 using the same T series turbo engine already planned for the 1993 220 Turbo Coupé and Rover 800 Vitesse. In the first six months of 1995, these new models accounted for 20 per cent of 600 sales, thereby successfully increasing overall volume and raising profitability.

Another improvement initiated to add value to the product was to address increasing customer choice but without reducing the effectiveness of the batch production process. Certain commonly specified options could be added randomly within the batches of thirty as long as they did not involve components sourced from Japan and affected relatively few other parts. An air conditioning system was therefore developed which met these criteria and, during 1994, a sunroof was also made available as an option on every model. At the same time the range of paint colours was increased from the initial five to six then to eight at the end of 1994 and again to eleven at the end of 1995. As customers were prepared to pay extra for air conditioning, sunroof and most of the new paint colours, all these actions significantly improved margins.

However, perhaps the most significant action taken to improve the profitability of the product was the gradual re-sourcing of expensive systems and sub-assemblies to Europe. This allowed more cost effective designs to be introduced and avoided the problems caused by the rising value of the yen as well as supporting Rover's traditional supply base. In collaboration with Honda, this enabled both companies to share in the cost of, for example, new anti-lock braking systems and power assisted steering designs, thereby further increasing both margins and local content.

Summary

This case study has highlighted a number of key issues in the development of a complex product. It has demonstrated some of the advantages to be gained from a joint venture between compatible organizations, it has indicated the way in which both real and perceived value can be added to an existing product by the careful selection and modification of key elements, and it has also shown how, through the identification of key project objectives and formulation of clear product, marketing, design and manufacturing strategies, all the varied activities can be successfully coordinated to develop a high quality product. Furthermore, examples of the importance of ensuring that additional product variants to address well understood sub-divisions of the market are made available within two years of initial launch, designing for the identified customers and seeking means of decreasing piece costs and thereby increasing profitability are all in evidence.

Epilogue

The success of the Rover 600 in taking on BMW, Audi and Mercedes had a number of repercussions. Together with updates to the 200, 400 and 800, the volume of both domestic and European sales achieved and the quality of the product raised the profile and reputation of the company to such an extent that in 1994 BMW bought Rover Group from British Aerospace. This move signalled an end to the partnership with Honda which, although not affecting the development of the 1995 400 series, would jeopardize the possibility of future collaborative products, leaving Honda to pursue its European car design and manufacture independently.

However, for Rover and BMW, this new situation would allow both companies to benefit from each other. The cooperation with Honda had helped Rover to implement quality systems, improve engineering and productivity. Nevertheless, having developed a product which successfully competed with BMW, Audi and Mercedes products, Rover now needed to learn more about a new approach to marketing products orientated more towards this specialist sector than the traditional areas of operation. The relationship with BMW would help Rover in moving further up the prestige ladder and learn an approach based more on knowing exactly what the customer wants and designing to that standard. In addition, unlike British Aerospace, BMW both have a detailed knowledge of the motor industry at a strategic as well as operational level and also have the money available to invest more in future products and support development. For BMW, who at the time had a relatively inefficient production facility, regularly incorporating rework, and therefore had much to learn about being right first time, the knowledge and experience of high quality, zero defect lean manufacture which Rover had acquired from Honda would provide a useful resource for their future development and growth.

How well this new relationship will benefit Rover in the future and whether it will prove to be as much of an advantage to them as the fifteen-year partnership with Honda remains to be seen but, given the company's developing product range and the ever changing market in which their vehicles are sold, it is clear that it should at least consolidate if not advance the progress already made.

2　Innovation

Innovate:	To change a thing into something new; to alter, to renew, to bring in something new for the first time; to introduce as new.
Innovation:	The action of innovating; the introduction of novelties; the alteration of what is established by the introduction of new elements or form. A change made in the nature or fashion of anything; something newly introduced; a novel practice or method etc. (*Oxford English Dictionary*)

Introduction

The success of a new product depends on many varied aspects of its design, its manufacture, its promotion and its distribution. In addition, issues such as the organization, resourcing and management of the development process through which it was developed, the quality and price of the products against which it may be competing in the marketplace and external influences such as prevailing market trends, legislation and environmental concerns can all affect its performance. However, there has always been one other feature that can be considered to have made as significant a contribution as any other to the build-up of a demand for a product. That feature is innovation. Whether a new product offers the user advantages over the existing model is a major influence in determining whether to purchase. Price and quality clearly have their part to play in this decision, but central to any customer's desire to buy is the belief that this new product will enable whatever task it performs or aids to be undertaken more effectively.

Consider for example the compact disc. When CD players were first launched in 1983 they offered little improvement in build quality over turntables and cassette decks, generally cost well over five times the price and yet millions were sold throughout the world. Even though the medium retailed was twice as expensive as the existing records and tapes, it rapidly grew in popularity, primarily because it was innovative. Commercially, far more successful than the subsequent DAT, MiniDisc and Digital Cassette formats, the CD offered a number of significant improvements over what had gone before: there was little or no distortion, there were no stylus or tape heads to wear out, the compact discs were smaller and easier to use than records, could not be scratched or de-magnetized and were also elegantly packaged. Similarly the transistor radio, the colour television, the jet engine and the motor car all offered clear advantages over what had gone before. The key element present in each of these which gave their respective purchasers the belief that they were more reliable, faster or more comfortable than preceding products, and hence the desire to own one stemmed from the fact that they were all clearly innovations over what had come before.

At its core new product development is based on innovation, an improvement on what already exists and, when you assess most successful products, somewhere within their success there is usually innovation at play. Sometimes it may be a production innovation such as a new way of moulding a component that means that a product can be manufactured more cheaply than before; sometimes it may be a marketing innovation such as an imaginative advertising campaign that results in greater awareness of the product; sometimes it can be an organizational innovation such as the development of telephone based insurance services which, by cutting out brokers, enabled more competitive premiums to be offered, and sometimes it may be a design innovation that means that the product itself is felt to be superior.

It is this last area that is the primary focus here, for although innovation in manufacturing and marketing are both evidently influential in a product's success, as far as the area of new product development is concerned, innovation in its design is usually the more directly significant. This chapter explains the difference between invention and innovation and indicates why the ability to innovate is significant to manufacturers' success. The options of innovating internally or sourcing innovation from outside the organization are both discussed. The reasons for protecting the intellectual property associated with an innovation are addressed and the varied means of achieving such protection are outlined.

Invention

It is important from the start to make a clear differentiation between innovation and invention. Invention is the creation of something completely new to the world which is not based on the development of an existing product, process or system. The light bulb, the telephone, the digital watch, the camera, the biro and the ring-pull beer can are all inventions; however it could be argued that, in their own right, the mountain bike, the colour television and graphite squash rackets are not. They can be considered as innovative developments of existing products, for at the time they were first developed, none could strictly be said to be entirely new products. Invention is often present in product development but not always, for invention is a component of innovation and therefore is also only part of the innovation process. Unfortunately many fail to appreciate this and fail to recognize the demands involved in developing an invention into a profitable product.

Over the years the British have become renowned for invention but this has not necessarily been accompanied by an ability to innovate – something more likely to be associated with the US or Japan. The microwave oven was invented in England in 1947, however it has been Japanese electrical companies such as Sharp, Matsushita and Korean manufacturer Samsung who have used innovation to develop the concept and manufacture high quality, high performance derivative products that are now sold all over the world. Similarly it was engineers at EMI in London who in 1972 invented the CAT scanner, but it is organizations like General Electric in the USA and Toshiba in Japan who have taken the technology, developed it and incorporated the original invention into the innovative scanning and imaging machines now found in most major hospitals.

Therefore when discussing innovation, it is important to remember that, although an invention may be present, it is not implicitly required and it is the capability to harness an invention, develop it and incorporate it within an innovative product that is the key commercial issue. It is not only a matter of having the imagination to dream up new ideas and the ability to solve identified problems, but also having the knowledge of how to turn the resulting conceptual solutions into well designed, well manufactured, well marketed products that makes the difference. Innovative organizations such as Sony and 3M which successfully use invention as part of the innovation process have demonstrated consistent growth over past years, but companies such as Thorn EMI, now basically a combination of music publishing, retailing and rental organizations, have not capitalized on the inventions which they originally nurtured and, as a result, have been unable to compete in their established markets and subsequently now have little presence in the field of manufacturing industry.

Innovation

Innovation can essentially be considered to occur successfully at two different levels, often termed 'breakthrough' and 'incremental'. Breakthrough or high innovation is most commonly associated with jumps, significant changes in a product or process, usually driven either by technology or design, sometimes incorporating a new invention and sometimes not. On the other hand, incremental or low innovation, the gradual improvement of a product through a series of steps or product variants, is most frequently characterized as small changes in, or development of, an existing design.

When the Sony Walkman was first launched in 1982 it was a break-through, a radical change in the concept of tape recorders. However since then, as more and more new models have been developed, the innovation that has taken place from one variant to the next has been incremental. The development of the waterproof Sports Walkman, the recording Walkman, Walkmans with integral AM and FM radios, noise reduction systems, anti-roll mechanisms and the consistent reduction in size, number of components and manufacturing costs, have all each been incremental innovations, steady improvements of the original breakthrough model.

Likewise when UK domestic appliance manufacturer GEC-Redring introduced the first plastic jug kettle, this too was a breakthrough. The use of a new, inexpensive material able to withstand boiling water enabled the realization of the concept of a lightweight, upright kettle which offered significant advantages over the conventional steel and aluminium models. But, as other manufacturers developed their own versions, each in turn used incremental innovation to improve on the previous model and continuously offer the customer a better and better product: the incorporation of external water level indicators and the improvement in material to overcome colour degradation were subsequently followed by inclusion of integral filters and the development of cordless models.

Of the two types, incremental innovation is certainly the most common alternative and consequently perceived by some to be the most successful. Through the development of a range of products over a period of time, technological, material, ergonomic and other design innovations can occur gradually, continuously improving the product and usually increasing or at least maintaining its market share. It is the safer option and using it effectively can be a lucrative strategy for a manufacturer.

Matsushita, known more outside Japan by their National and Panasonic brand names, are one of the most profitable Japanese electronics companies. Although they are rarely seen to deliver a breakthrough innovation, by constantly developing incrementally improved products such as mobile phones and video recorders, two areas in which they launch many new models every year, they are able continuously to track the market and always have a variant available with all the latest features selling at a competitive price. Although in order to achieve significant profitability they have both to overcome the innovator's head start and associated market share and also reduce manufacturing costs to a competitive level, by doing so repeatedly they have been able consistently to provide users with the latest technology within an appropriate package to such an extent that they are now the world's largest electronics manufacturer.-

However, although generally considered to be a greater risk, the rewards that stand to be obtained from breakthrough innovation can be far more significant. By making a big leap forward, a manufacturer can gain a clearly identifiable lead over the competition and, if this lead is maintained, the increased market share or brand superiority that is usually acquired initially can be sustained for a long time. Together Philips and Sony, co-inventors of the compact disc, still dominate the supply of the key components, Hewlett

Packard continue to lead the laser printer market and Pilkington, who developed the float glass method of glass production, almost control an entire industrial sector.

Nevertheless, it must be recognized that whilst the initial breakthrough can provide a substantial demand at first, if a company fails to continuously incrementally improve the original invention, there is always the risk that other companies may take over a large share of the market. IBM failed to maintain their lead in the personal computer field, thus allowing companies such as Compaq to overtake them; Redring did not build upon their initial innovation in kettle design, allowing companies such as Tefal and Rowenta to now lead the market and, arguably, until the launch of the Discovery, Land Rover were slow to develop new models, permitting Japanese manufacturers such as Suzuki, Toyota and Mitsubishi to build up a large share of the four-wheel drive vehicle market. However companies such as Sony with the Walkman, JCB with back-hoe excavators and the likes of Nike and Reebok in sports footwear have continuously developed new products and as a result are still leaders in their individual fields.

Whilst there is no simple formula for making the best use of innovation, organizations which make a breakthrough and continuously improve upon it to maintain their lead and companies which, although not the original inventors, constantly develop new versions each offering better performance or value for money than the previous ones, both tend to survive and prosper. However companies which either fail to capitalize upon their innovation or simply imitate others' products are, in the long term, less likely to thrive: with few exceptions every product eventually becomes obsolete and therefore organizations which do not innovate frequently become vulnerable to competition from more efficient manufacturers able to produce better and cheaper products.

Internal innovation

Although innovation can occur in any of the marketing, sales, manufacturing, finance and management environments, within most organizations the core areas in which it is actively encouraged and expected are the design and development activities and particularly R&D. Technological innovation is a key element of successful product development and ensuring that it occurs effectively is a major concern for many companies.

At its heart internal innovation relies on the organization possessing four basic capabilities:

- the ability to identify market opportunities,
- the capacity to generate new ideas,
- the means to research problems and identify potential solutions, and
- the skills to develop these solutions into proven product concepts.

Enabling this requires not only the right combination of creative and analytical individuals within the organization, but also the necessary physical and organizational resources that together allow innovation to occur.

As well as ensuring that the appropriate equipment and facilities are made available, from a financial perspective, these resources include the provision of a clear annual investment in R&D, sufficient to enable the necessary activities to occur, and a long term commitment to innovation which is made with full awareness of the particular demands of innovation and its incompatibility with short termism.

The most significant attributes from a management point of view are direction and focus, for without these the investment may deliver few rewards. By its very nature the innovation process is difficult both to predict and control. Not only may the unexpected results of, say, a series of experiments necessitate the pursuit of alternative solutions, but the intrinsic creative thinking involved in R&D might easily shift into other parallel areas. Therefore, to achieve a beneficial result from R&D within reasonable time frames, many organizations have continuously to monitor the direction and progress of individual programmes and ensure that they maintain a focus on the key target problems.

In conjunction with these, another key ingredient to successful internal innovation lies in the development and maintenance of a culture to support it. As well as the creation of a climate which encourages innovation, perhaps through the use of varied creative techniques such as brainstorming and the adoption of financial and non-financial reward systems, the more successful innovating companies also ensure that the right environment is fostered. Typically informal, this often relies on individual or group autonomy, toleration of occasional conflict and continuous personal and corporate learning from failure.

3M

3M, the Minnesota-based multinational manufacturer has become renowned for its internal innovation capabilities. Now comprising forty divisions producing 60,000 products utilizing 130 different technologies, over the years the company has grown and refined its product development activities to a level where it regularly achieves a corporate objective of generating 25 per cent of turnover from products introduced in the last five years. To enable this to take place 3M not only provides all the required physical and financial resources for new research programmes to be undertaken, but also creates an environment and culture within which they occur. This is common across the company and is based on four key principles:

● Organizationally each division has a high level of autonomy and is able to develop ideas through internal venture groups. This ensures that the necessary finance and equipment is provided for each project.

- Across all divisions, there is shared access to all existing technologies so that individual projects can easily draw on and adopt techniques or processes that have been developed for other applications. This helps the company maximize the use of each of its core technologies.
- There is a company policy to guarantee all technical researchers the opportunity to spend up to 15 per cent of their time on projects of their own choosing. These need have no connection with current or previous 3M products but are nevertheless supported by the company as a key means of generating innovative ideas. Individual inventors whose ideas prove feasible also have the opportunity of then taking them right through to production.
- There are separate career paths for innovators with a dual ladder system ensuring that R&D personnel are not forced into management roles as the only means of promotion, but are able to continue in their field with equal remuneration and responsibility.

Together these are implemented throughout the organization and over the years have helped it to develop, manufacture and market such a wide range of successful products including adhesives, reflective tapes, post-it notes, inhalers and data storage devices.

External innovation

As an alternative to undertaking the initial research and development of a new product internally, many companies prefer to use external organizations. Universities, trade research associations and bespoke consultancies all offer manufacturers the capability of having specific research and product development projects undertaken outside. By commissioning organizations who may either already have the necessary facilities required to undertake the particular experimentation or testing of concepts, or employ personnel with specialized knowledge in the particular field in which the innovation is planned to occur, manufacturers can often obtain highly productive research which can be beneficial for both large multinationals and smaller manufacturers.

Having the early research work sub-contracted to specialist organizations means that the manufacturers themselves can concentrate on the development of the chosen device or process into a manufacturable product, without the need to support internal R&D activities. In many instances, where the programmes are carefully planned, professionally undertaken and regularly monitored, this approach can lead to the generation of highly successful innovations. However, this should not be viewed as a cheap option nor one to necessarily replace the role of R&D within the company.

Another option available to manufacturers, is the acquisition of existing innovation from outside. Either on a business-to-business basis or through individual inventors, many organizations seek and acquire new technology and new products by licensing them from the originators. At one extreme there are companies like Philips who with Sony, have successfully used their patent protection relating to compact discs to license their manufacture to all the other main consumer electronics manufacturers. At the other end of the scale, there are cases such as the Workmate which was originally invented and developed by Ron Hickman, an automotive engineer at Lotus, and eventually licensed to DIY products manufacturer Black and Decker. In both situations the original inventors benefit by receiving royalties on products made in far greater volumes than they could individually have supported, and the companies acquiring the technology or product also gain, firstly, by being able to manufacture and sell a new product in volume and, secondly, by doing so without funding all the initial R&D.

Many manufacturing companies wish both to strengthen and broaden their product range. If some other organization or individual has developed an innovation which can either be applied to their existing products to improve their performance, increase their reliability or decrease their cost, or alternatively, can become the basis for a new family of products complementary to their existing ones, then there are clear advantages to be gained from either licensing or buying it outright. Primarily this means not only that an innovative new product can be acquired directly without the need to undertake the research internally, but also that, by acquiring it, the company can prevent a rival from developing it as a competitive product.

In the successful acquisition of products from outside the organization a problem frequently faced by both the original sources of the innovations and the companies who wish to acquire them is making contact and finding either the right product or the right manufacturer. There are three options available:

- The first and perhaps the most common alternative is for the originator, whether it be an individual or a company, to identify and approach what are seen to be potential licensees. By systematically working through existing manufacturers of similar products and organizations who may wish to extend their product range to include the innovation, an interested company can occasionally be found and, after much negotiation, the innovation may be licensed and manufactured. However, the chances of this happening are extremely slight and, although illustrated by the accompanying Flymo Gardenvac example, very few manage to find a sufficiently interested organization.
- From the opposite direction, manufacturers themselves can undertake patent searches. Every month over 1000 patent applications are published in the UK alone and world wide the figure is over ten times this. All of these published applications are available either at a patent office or via on-line facilities found in libraries, universities and sometimes within companies themselves. By conducting a patent search of a specified field of interest, manufacturers can assess whether there are any innovations which might be appropriate for acquisition and, by subscribing to a patent watch, can regularly scan recently published patents to keep track of developments in particular areas. Such facilities can greatly assist companies in quickly identifying products which may possibly be licensed.

- Third, there are a growing number of companies set up as technology transfer organizations, some of which have been operating internationally for many years and others which are relatively smaller scale localized operations. All ideally seek to match the best ideas with the most appropriate manufacturers. Some, such as the British Technology Group, who have traditionally acted as a conduit for inventions from university and government research establishments, not only act as a go-between but often finance both the development of product concepts and assist with patenting. However, the majority concentrate more on inter-corporate licensing and the business-to-business transfer of innovation. All are now beginning also to take more of an interest in new products from individual inventors and designers.

Whichever route is taken, the organizations which acquire the right to develop a new product gain the combined advantages of:

- by-passing much of the costly and uncertain R&D effort,
- selecting only product concepts which have close synergy with their product range, and
- significantly reducing internal development periods.

Intellectual property

Whether innovation occurs within the organization or outside, a critical issue associated with all products and technology is the ownership of the associated intellectual property. To both take advantage of an innovation and also prevent others from copying it, the vast majority of manufacturers seek to formally protect their ideas, concepts and designs and, to achieve

Table 2.1 Types of intellectual property protection

Protection	Subject
Patent	A new product or process that is inventive and capable of industrial application
Design right	A new design product
Registered design	A new product which is aesthetically original
Copyright	An original piece of writing, drawing, music, a film, a recording or a computer program
Trade mark	An identification symbol which is used to distinguish one specific product from other similar products
Service mark	An identification symbol which is used to distinguish one specific service from other similar services

this, they declare and legally protect the intellectual property (Table 2.1) associated with the innovation. Patents, design rights, registered designs, copyright, trademarks and service marks all play an important part in the protection of ideas and designs. They give legal recognition to the ownership of new ideas, designs or brand-names enabling them to be treated as a commodity and also give the owners the right to stop other people or companies exploiting what is their property. They create a system by which the innovators themselves can benefit, be it from the invention of the digital watch, the design of a pair of jeans, the name of a drink or the writing of a novel or piece of music.

Detailed guidance (Patent Office, 1996/Nabarro Nathanson, 1994) is available on the appropriate method for the protection of intellectual property on an individual basis, but the scope of each with respect to products can generally be summarized.

Patent

A patent is the strongest form of protection available for an innovation because it protects the essence of the invention and the patentee obtains a monopoly legal right to use, license or assign it as he or she wishes. Lasting up to twenty years from the date of filing, this protection gives both monopoly and security wherever a patent is granted. Virtually all machines, products or processes and the individual parts of them across the industrial spectrum are patentable provided they satisfy three criteria; they must be new, they must be inventive and they must be capable of industrial application. An outline of the patenting process in the UK is represented in Figure 2.1.

Design right

Design right automatically protects all aspects of the shape and configuration of a product as soon as it is either designed or made. As long as the design is original and has not been copied from another, the design right provides up to ten years' protection against direct copying of a product. Although the design right requires no formal application and occurs naturally, it is not a monopoly and does not cover the independent generation of the same product.

Registered design

Registering a design is, like patenting, a positive act providing protection for a novel design. This does not however cover any feature dictated solely by the product's function but addresses the visual aspects of the shape of the product. It is a monopoly and consequently covers both direct copies and similar products generated independently. Although not providing the level of protection obtainable from a patent, this does therefore enable greater cover than the automatic design right.

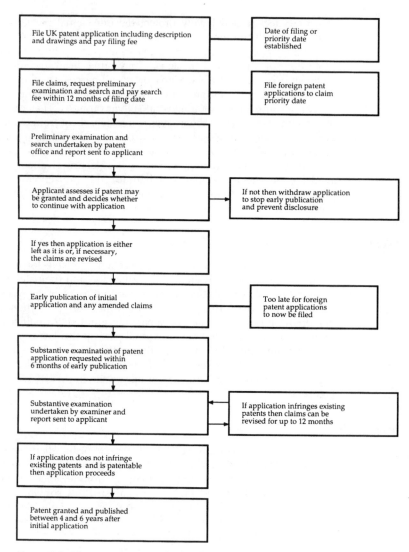

Figure 2.1 The patent process in the UK

Copyright

Whereas copyright is usually associated with literary and artistic works, this automatic protection, which lasts fifty years after the death of the originator, does have applications in product development. Not only does it provide additional protection for drawings, product specifications and manuals, but it also covers any specifically written computer software. In addition it also protects any surface decoration applied to the product which has been specifically created for it.

Trademarks

Registration of a trademark which may be a word, logo or symbol, provides an exclusive licence to use it for any goods for which it is registered. Thus this protection prevents manufacturers from producing products which adopt similar logos to those registered by their originators. Easily prosecuted for infringement, trademarks therefore prevent counterfeiting and unfair competition.

Service marks

A service mark is a word, logo or symbol registered for use with a particular service rather than a product. Providing the same level of protection as a trademark, this correspondingly prevents other organizations from replicating of, for example, retail outlets, distribution centres and maintenance facilities and therefore ensures that products are only sold and repaired by agents approved by the manufacturer.

International protection

Whilst for some products, it may only be necessary to obtain protection for the domestic market, for the majority, most of which are either sold abroad or face foreign competition, it is best also to gain protection internationally. Although also applicable to design registration, copyright and trade and service marks, the most widely utilized form of international protection for new products is not surprisingly the patent. Whilst the majority of nations operate their own individual patent offices granting protection on a country by country basis, there are two organizations which coordinate protection over a number of countries. The European Patent Office in Munich acts as a central filing facility for all European countries whilst a PCT filing allows simultaneous patent applications to be filed virtually worldwide. Although both require the individual countries for which protection is desired to be specified, they enable all the necessary documentation to be dealt with centrally and greatly simplify the process.

Finally, whilst many organizations patent inventions which they themselves seek to manufacture, some do so with the intention of also licensing the intellectual property. Universities, research organizations and a number of bespoke product development companies all use patents as the key means of not only protecting their inventions but also as a facility for commercializing their work. Either on a business-to-business basis or from a sole inventor, the ability to license a patent or any other form of intellectual property can have many benefits. The examples of compact discs and the Workmate both show how companies such as Philips and Black and Decker and individual innovators have used licensing as a key part of their ability to develop products.

Although negotiable in each application, an inventor typically grants sole or multiple licences to one or more manufacturers to develop and produce products based on his or her invention in specified markets. In return the inventor receives either a lump sum payment or, more often, a royalty usually defined as a percentage of product cost, profit or turnover. This system allows both parties to benefit. Manufacturers gain access to a new product or technology with which they can generate income for themselves and the inventor receives a share, hopefully representative of his contribution.

Chapter summary

This chapter has addressed some of the issues associated with innovation in product development. It has explained the difference between invention and innovation and discussed why innovation is so important to ongoing success. The two alternative approaches to innovation have been identified and their relative merits outlined. The options of innovating internally or externally have both been discussed and the different means of acquiring innovation from outside the organization have been described. Finally the roles of creating, owning and licensing the intellectual property associated with an innovation have been covered and brief descriptions of the different types of such protection have been identified. The key issues addressed in this chapter can therefore be summarized as:

- Innovation has a major role in product development and is frequently highly influential in a product's commercial success.
- Invention, the creation of something totally new, is only a part of the innovation process and does not necessarily have to be present.
- High level breakthrough innovation is associated with big jumps in either technology or design of a product or process. Although high risk, the rewards can be significant.
- Low level incremental innovation is characterized as small changes in or development of an existing design. As the safer option, this is the most commonly adopted approach.
- Internal innovation relies on the organization possessing a number of key capabilities, supported by necessary resources and a creative climate.
- External innovation can enable organizations to out-source the early creative stages of product development, potentially improving effectiveness and reducing costs.
- Innovation in any area can be protected and exploited through the appropriate creation and administration of intellectual property.

References

Drucker, P.F. (1986) *Innovation and Entrepreneurship*. Pan Books, London.
European Patent Office (1994) *How to get a European Patent*. European Patent Office, Munich.
Nabarro Nathanson (1994) *A Legal Guide to Innovation*. Nabarro Nathanson, London.
Patent Office (1996) *How to Prepare a UK Patent Application*. Patent Office, Cardiff Road, Newport, Wales.
West, A. (1992) *Innovation Strategy*. Prentice Hall International, London.
Yates, I. (1992) *Innovation, Investment and Survival of the UK Economy*. The Royal Academy of Engineering, London.

Case study 2: Flymo Gardenvac

Flymo is a UK based manufacturer of garden products. Since 1964 the company has developed an innovative product range comprising electric and petrol driven hover mowers, wheeled rotary mowers, lawn trimmers, hedge-trimmers and, from spring 1993, the Gardenvac (Figure C2.1). As part of the multinational Electrolux organization since 1968, their products are now sold in Europe, the United States, South Africa, Australia and the Far East, generating an annual turnover in 1994 of £95m. Their main competitors in the UK garden product market are Qualcast and Black and Decker with whom they share 90 per cent of lawnmower sales.

The majority of their products all share core cutting technology and are generally sold during the spring and summer months. In the late 1980s the Flymo/Electrolux group investigated the potential market available for other garden care products, and, following detailed research, focused on the

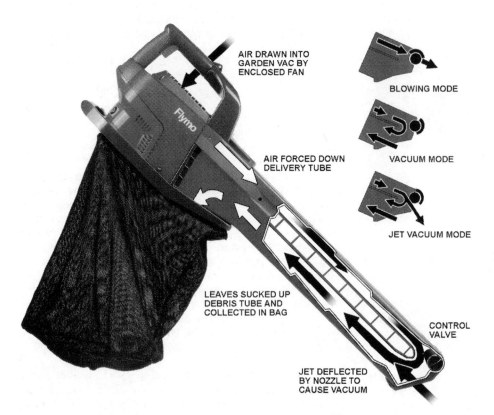

AIR DRAWN INTO
GARDEN VAC BY
ENCLOSED FAN

BLOWING MODE

AIR FORCED DOWN
DELIVERY TUBE

VACUUM MODE

JET VACUUM MODE

LEAVES SUCKED UP
DEBRIS TUBE AND
COLLECTED IN BAG

CONTROL
VALVE

JET DEFLECTED
BY NOZZLE TO
CAUSE VACUUM

Figure C2.1 Flymo Gardenvac. Reproduced by kind permission of Flymo Limited consumer demand for a garden 'tidy' product. Specifically they identified the need for an easy to use, competitively priced, all-purpose tool that could clear leaves, collect litter and tidy up trimmings from hedges and lawn borders.

During the 1980s there had been a significant growth in the sales of conventional blowers in the United States. Brands such as McCulloch, Homelite, Black and Decker and Poulan-Weedeater, also part of the Electrolux group, helped expand the market over the decade to over 2 million units per annum. By 1990 it was apparent to Electrolux and, as part of the same group, Flymo, that the UK garden tidy market was therefore one of significant untapped potential and the 'blowervac' product category could easily be developed to rival the size of other garden care market sectors.

Not only would adding such a product increase Flymo's existing product range, but it would also give them a counter seasonal product which would extend their period of sales into the autumn months. However, to enter this market, they had to choose between either importing and branding an existing US product or manufacturing their own. If they were to take the second route, they could either design a new product themselves or, alternatively, acquire an innovative product from outside the company and then develop it internally. They chose the latter option.

This case history describes the invention and design of an innovative garden tidy product by a sole individual, its acquisition by an established manufacturer, its subsequent development and successful launch onto the market.

The idea

In autumn 1989 John Coathupe was a senior training officer in the north west of England, supervising engineering apprenticeships in companies throughout the region. At that time he owned one of the original Flymo hover mowers which, although proficient at cutting grass, would also blow the cut grass not just onto his lawn but also onto the drive and onto the soil where it was difficult to pick up. In addition, as many of the leaves from the trees in his garden were small, they were very difficult to brush up and, in the wet, were frequently walked inside the house. To help him keep his garden tidy he therefore looked for a product which would pick up such debris but could not find one: although traditional blower products were being manufactured and sold in the US, at that time they were not readily available in Europe. Therefore, unaware of the existing US machines, he started to think how leaves and grass cuttings could be most efficiently collected.

His knowledge of conventional vacuum cleaners identified two specific characteristics of interest:

● Whenever the nozzle of a hose attachment come into contact with a surface it 'snatches'. If used outside this would clearly lead to problems as, if such a nozzle were to come too close to the ground, it would not only pick up grass cuttings and leaves but also unwanted soil and gravel.

● If too much debris is picked up at once, the hose frequently becomes blocked at the mouth. This too would also be an undesirable feature for a product which should be capable of clearing up large volumes of leaves and grass cuttings.

Assessing the two main types of vacuum cleaners available, it was recognized that with cylinder models, air is drawn through a dirt collecting bag and then passes through the guts of the machine, subsequently flowing out of the rear of the product. Since a collecting bag must be contained within an airtight cylinder, if this system were to be adapted for use in the garden then the developed product would probably be large and heavy and therefore not very portable. With the other type of conventional vacuum, most commonly seen in upright cleaners, material first flows through a fan and is then blown into a bag. In this case the bag does not need to be contained within an airtight chamber and is often attached to the outside of the device. However, if a product based on this principle were to be used in the garden, problems were likely to be encountered with the fan jamming as not only leaves but other less compressible debris such as twigs and litter were also picked up.

Experimentation

Although neither of these existing products offered a ready-made solution, it was clear to John that moving air was going to be the best means of collecting grass and leaves, and so he experimented with blowing air into a tube and trying to induce secondary airflow through it. His first model used two pieces of sanitary piping – a small section connected to a larger diameter length at an acute angle. The blowing output of an old conventional Electrolux vacuum cleaner was connected to the smaller section to provide a primary airflow. This induced a small secondary flow in the larger pipe, which enabled small dry leaves successfully to be picked up. There was however insufficient suction to cope with larger volumes of leaves and grass cuttings and so, to perform the desired tasks better, it was evident that larger section tubing and increased airflow would be required.

His second model was therefore based around a piece of plastic drainpipe and a 3-litre Coke bottle. Using a similar feed pipe as before from the vacuum cleaner, air was fed into the bottle, which acted as a plenum chamber and from which four tubes directed the airflow back up the central pipe. Unfortunately the performance was similar to the first model and it became clear that to make this principle work effectively it would be necessary to significantly increase the volume of air flowing through the main tube. Although this would create the required suction, it would also present a new problem of what to do with all the exhaust air: if it was to be blown into a collecting bag, which would have to be of a relatively close weave to collect the debris, not only might the bag be blown up like a balloon but air may also flow back down the tube. Faced with this problem, it was therefore time for a reappraisal of precisely what the aim was.

After some thought, the crux of the solution became apparent: the high speed airflow should occur not part way up the main tube, but at the mouth, for it had to be as near as possible to whatever was to be picked up. As discovered by the Swiss mathematician David Bernoulli in 1738, when the velocity of an airflow is increased, its pressure correspondingly reduces. Therefore, if high speed air is blown between two surfaces, anything lying loose on the surfaces will be drawn into the airflow. If this principle could be achieved at the mouth of the tube then debris could be more easily attracted into the main airflow. With leaves and grass cuttings thus within the airflow, another natural phenomenon, known as the Coanda effect, could also be utilized: whenever a fluid flows over or near a curved or inclined surface, a partial vacuum is formed, and the fluid tends to 'stick' to the surface and flow round it. This can be most easily seen as water from a tap clings to a finger placed in its path. Thus, by directing the airflow parallel to the ground, and positioning a controlling surface at the nozzle to encourage this effect, the air and the accumulated grass and leaves should flow round the mouth and up, along the inside wall of the tube.

Although the ideal was to create a bell-shaped nozzle with air coming down the outside and being forced in all around, John knew that this would be difficult to construct. Instead, to enable simple evaluation of the idea, two panels were cut in an old dishwasher powder carton, one each in the front and back. These were both folded inwards creating a curve at the bottom of the container and a section of 20-mm tube was attached to produce another model. This time the tube was plugged at one end and had a number of small holes pierced in a line along its length. By positioning these air holes in close proximity to the curved bottom panel and again connecting the vacuum cleaner output, a stream of high speed air flowed over this 'control surface'. This new model was tested on a bench covered in pieces of tissue and plastic shreds, with the immediate result of all the debris being caught by the airflow and blown straight through the channel in the carton, clearly demonstrating that this was the kernel of a potentially realistic solution. The model was then taken outside on a cold and wet November evening and tried out again, this time on the more difficult subject of leaves floating on a puddle of water. Again it worked well with the leaves being picked out of the water as the model was gently passed over the surface.

As it was now clear that a credible solution was possible, a range of different models were then made to explore this principle of blowing a stream of high speed air over a control surface, located as near to the mouth of the main tube as possible in order to create the suction required to pick up grass, leaves and twigs. By experimenting with different shapes and curves it was not really possible to accurately measure the subtle differences between them. However, it was evident from the performance of these models that the area of the mouth could be increased without increasing the size of the power unit and the same effect could still be achieved. This was a clear advantage over the still unknown conventional blowervac products made in the US which all had a fan at the top, drawing air up a tube, and a collection bag attached behind. But, since their main tubes are generally in excess of

100 mm in diameter, to achieve the necessary airflow far more powerful fans than those used in vacuum cleaners are required – whereas here the desired effect was being achieved using a standard size unit.

To ascertain the potential performance that might be available from the real product John next built a full size prototype, and, to make it easy to model, adopted a rectangular section duct and used primarily balsa wood. As the possibility of using the invention to pick up litter as well as grass cuttings and leaves was then realized, this prototype was designed to pick up a drinks can and scaled accordingly. It had two outlets, one at the front of the mouth blowing air parallel to the ground, giving the desired grasping action, and another at the rear blowing air over a second control surface and more directly into the main tube, which also gave some driving power to force debris up the tube and into the collecting bag. Although to create the airflow, the end product would have an integral motor located at the top of the main tube near to the handle, for simplicity, this prototype continued to use the now established external power supply of the vacuum cleaner.

Patenting and licensing

As the product was plainly highly innovative and could have significant market potential, it was quickly determined that it was necessary to protect it by filing a patent application. To clarify his understanding of the details of the patenting process, John had recently approached a patent agent for advice on what aspects of his invention could and could not be patented. Subsequently in February 1990 the prototype, drawings and descriptions of how it worked were taken to the patent agent, the specification drawn up and the patent application filed. This gave him a maximum of twelve months before the more costly applications for similar protection outside the UK would have to be made.

Having obtained the necessary protection for the invention, next came the decision of what was to be done with it. By now well aware of how innovative a product he had invented, John had to decide whether he was going to develop it further himself, perhaps even setting up a company to manufacture it, or whether to try to license it to an existing manufacturer. Given the significant resources required to manufacture, promote and distribute such a product, he chose the second option.

A number of suitable companies were identified and approached. These included established garden product companies such as Black and Decker, Qualcast and Mountfield and a selection of vacuum cleaner manufacturers such as Hoover and Vax. The Electrolux Group covered both these product areas, and were therefore approached directly at their main UK manufacturing facility in Newton Aycliffe, Durham. Six letters were written in March 1990 and replies soon came back from all, asking either for more information or for a demonstration of the product.

Over the next few weeks additional information was sent and the prototype was demonstrated to both Electrolux and Black and Decker. Initially

Electrolux saw this as a product which would be most appropriate in their Floor-care division, for, at the time it was felt that, as a vacuum cleaner for use outside, it would extend that division's existing product range into a new area, one which competing products from other companies were beginning to address. An invitation to demonstrate the product duly came from this division which was based in Luton. Taking along bags of polystyrene strips, dried leaves, grass cuttings, pieces of paper and crushed cans, all of which he knew would contribute to a necessarily convincing demonstration, John initially showed it to Geoff Brewin, product engineering manager and a few weeks later to the division's product review committee. In between these two demonstrations at Electrolux, the prototype was also taken to Black and Decker's outdoor products division in Spennymoor, and shown to the head of R&D at this facility.

Both companies were impressed by the performance of the prototype and were sufficiently interested in the product's potential to offer to develop it further and make some fully working prototypes. This led to the need to make a choice between the two, either of which was, from an external perspective, an ideal manufacturer for the product. This decision was not an easy one and the relative advantages of each alternative had to be carefully considered: Black and Decker were a highly regarded manufacturer of power tools, with a very strong presence in the international DIY market, whereas Electrolux was a successful multinational organization manufacturing a wide range of domestic and consumer products with two subsidiaries, Flymo and Weedeater, each having significant shares of the European and US garden-care product markets respectively. In the end the decision was made to go with Electrolux because whereas both organizations could potentially manufacture and market electric versions of the product, only the Electrolux group would also have the capacity to manufacture petrol driven versions, thereby, in John's opinion, offering a far wider and greater potential market for the product.

It was agreed that Electrolux Floor-care would undertake some market testing and examine how well the product could fit into the company's product range. In addition they would also make a number of development models to assess whether it was both technically feasible and manufacturable and also determine potential performance characteristics. This was done with the assistance of an external design group, who produced two working prototypes from thermoplastic sheeting. These incorporated motors at the top as initially planned, both to give the product the necessary balance and to improve the ergonomics by reducing any strain on the user. They also utilized airflow coming from only the front of the nozzle and not from the back, although the 'control surface' that had previously been used at the rear was now incorporated at the front to maintain the grasping and driving combination.

Unfortunately, in December 1990, after six months development and evaluation, Electrolux Floor-care decided not to go ahead with the project. Although they had confirmed that the product was technically viable and could potentially be manufactured at a realistic cost, after carrying out initial hall tests with the prototypes, they had reservations about its market potential. Fundamentally it was not felt to fit in with the rest of their portfolio of vacuuming products. Geoff Brewin however was convinced of the product's potential and emphasized that the rejection from Electrolux was only because of the poor results obtained from the market research. He therefore redirected the project to Flymo for evaluation as a garden only product and, in the meantime, gave both prototypes to John. The twelve months during which overseas patent applications could be filed were very nearly over and time was running out. John found himself in a difficult position: the expense of filing these applications himself would be considerable, but if they were not filed, the product would be of reduced value to a prospective manufacturer due to its limited protection.

In January 1991, he again approached Black and Decker to see if they were still interested. They were and repeated their offer to evaluate the prototypes. In addition, towards the end of 1990, details of the product had been sent to the British Technology Group, one of the UK's largest technology transfer companies. They responded positively and expressed a serious interest in the product: their usual offer was a share of all future royalties generated from licensing, but only if the intellectual property was assigned to them. This was an offer which had as many advantages as disadvantages. Given their experience and worldwide manufacturing contacts, the British Technology Group could potentially secure a very good deal with a number of different manufacturers in various countries, but in assigning the patent rights John would lose control of the product and have no part in its future development.

While John was weighing up these two options, Brian Wytcherly, product planning manager at Flymo asked for a demonstration. Following a recent assessment of the US market by Electrolux, Flymo had independently completed a survey of the potential for a garden tidy product in the European market and had been looking at a number of options. They were in the process of evaluating whether to brand one of the existing Electrolux owned Poulan-Weedeater products, develop an improved version of a US product to overcome an identified problem of clogging by wet leaves, or alternatively, develop their own new product for which a number of concepts had been generated internally. So, when the information about the Gardenvac – a 'clean fan' solution potentially better than existing 'dirty fan' US products – was passed across from the Floor-care division, Flymo were very keen to see it. Another demonstration took place at their facility in Newton Aycliffe, Durham in the last week of January after which strong interest in the product was expressed yet again.

So in February 1991, John faced another choice, now between three offers: from Black and Decker, the British Technology Group and Flymo. He chose the latter. Despite having already spent so much time with Electrolux Floor-care and even though the contact with Flymo was a recent one, Flymo represented the best option. The reasons were much the same as before: the range of products manufactured by the group meant that both petrol and electric versions were possible, offering greater potential for the product than with Black and Decker. In addition, although they had not acquired a product from outside since the first Flymo in 1965, Flymo were clearly very keen to back the product by providing all the necessary resources, funding its development and initiating an extensive high profile marketing campaign, all of which amounted to a £3m commitment. As for the BTG option, this would have meant effectively losing control of the product and, after his effort to date, John wanted to see the project through to conclusion. The invention was therefore licensed to Flymo and both the original balsa model and the prototypes made for Electrolux Floor-care were handed over for further development in February 1991.

Development

Over the next six months a number of different developments of the product took place within Flymo. The design was first assessed in detail from an ergonomic perspective with different configurations of the tube, handle and motor being evaluated to determine the optimum solution in terms of balance and ease of use. To further enhance this aspect of the product, the idea of incorporating a supporting shoulder strap to enable it to be used for extended period was evolved and included as an extra feature.

In addition, experiments were undertaken with different sizes and shapes of the nozzle. Before finalizing the design, Flymo wanted to determine what ratio between the cross-sectional areas of the delivery tube and debris tube was necessary to achieve optimal performance and what specific profile of the control surface provided the best suction. To assess this a whole range of models were produced and tested. During this development, the possibility of enabling the product to blow as well as vacuum was also discussed and the idea of using a rotating valve control at the end of the delivery tube suggested. Such a valve would, in one configuration, produce the existing vacuuming action and, in another, would allow the high speed air to flow directly out of the end of the delivery tube giving the product a blowing facility. This improvement was modelled, evaluated and following successful testing incorporated within the design.

Next an additional feature, the jet vacuum, was also introduced to overcome an identified problem with wet leaves. In damp conditions there is often a level of adhesion between leaves and smooth surfaces such as paths, patios and driveways which prevents them being picked up by the standard vacuum. However, by bleeding off a little air from the main flow in vacuum mode, a powerful jet of air flowing through a small slot in the control valve could be created. This would help to chisel or turn up the edges of any leaves, reducing the adhesion and consequently enabling the predominant flow of air up the debris channel to successfully pick up the leaves off the ground. Again after modelling and testing, this additional feature was also incorporated within the evolving product as a third setting on the control valve, thereby enabling users to easily switch from blowing to vacuum to jet vacuum.

The other key development work undertaken at this stage was the determination of precise power requirements and the sourcing of an appropriate motor. Although a standard vacuum cleaner power unit had been used in all the prototypes, it was felt that a more efficient fan would benefit the product's overall performance, and after a number of trials, a suitable motor was found. Sourced from Electrolux's main supplier for their vacuum cleaners, a standard sized product with a different wind on the motor proved capable of providing the desired output and was subsequently selected. This choice proved useful later when a version of the product for the US market was developed. Not only was a different voltage motor required but for market reasons an even more powerful output was also required. However, by using this standard sized product, the necessary additional winding could be simply incorporated within the same size cage and the motor would therefore fit into the same mountings as the European model.

In October 1991, the results of these assessments and the original prototypes were handed over to an internal development team whose responsibility it was to turn the working prototypes into a manufacturable product which met all the appropriate standards, could be easily assembled and would achieve the planned ex-works target cost thus enabling it to be sold for a desired £79. They had to bring together all the various developments into a single coherent product and, working within defined parameters, quickly produced initial drawings used to create another full size working prototype incorporating the control valve, the chosen power unit and the shoulder-strap facility.

Once this had been tested Flymo then involved an external industrial design consultancy, Renfrew Associates, to provide an input to the styling of the product. Although the key dimensions were by now well defined and mounting and interlock details were being determined in house, the industrial designers at Renfrew were able to work on the overall external shape to produce a design which would both enhance market perceptions of an innovative product and fit into the developing Flymo product range. They defined all the external surfaces, colour and textures and by the end of January 1992 had produced a full scale mock-up of the proposed design (Figure C2.2). Moulded in ABS, it would be predominantly smooth and orange, the established Flymo corporate colour, with a grey textured handle, motor casing, control valve and mouthpiece.

The product would be assembled from seven major and five minor mouldings for which the in-house team next set about preparing drawings. Working from their own data, the new model and accompanying drawings from Renfrew Associates, they produced all the necessary drawings and passed them to the selected toolmaker in May 1992. Whereas the company now use 3D modelling and rapid prototyping and tooling facilities, at this time Flymo were still using the traditional pattern making method of toolmaking which meant that initial wax shots were not available until the end of the year. But, as soon as these were received, they were checked against the original drawings and, following approval, the tools were subsequently transferred to the main Electrolux production facility, adjacent to Flymo, where sampling in ABS started in January 1993.

Figure C2.2 Flymo Gardenvac. Reproduced by kind permission of Flymo Limited

The first samples were used by the development team to build initial products to evaluate product performance and check that all the mouldings fitted within planned tolerances. Further mouldings were then used for a pre-production build by manufacturing to test their assembly line in February, leading to the commencement of full scale production in March 1993, thus allowing the UK launch within ten weeks of receipt of the tools.

Product performance

At the time of its launch in March 1993, the UK market for conventional blowervacs imported from the US was only 5000 units a year. Within six months Flymo were selling this many a week and by the end of the first year had sold 200,000. They had invested in a high profile TV advertising campaign which together with a valuable free demonstration on the BBC's Tomorrow's World programme helped sales and rapidly led to the Gardenvac becoming a generic name for garden tidy products just as Hoover had previously done for vacuum cleaners.

In reaction to this success, Black and Decker quickly imported and re-engineered one of their existing traditional US products to compete in the UK market but were unable to catch up with Flymo who, having successfully persuaded Weedeater to factor the Gardenvac as a premium product in the USA and Canada, by mid-1995 had sold over 1,000,000 units worldwide. It became Flymo's number one selling product in the UK, accounting for 10 per cent of the company turnover and was critical in helping to reposition Flymo as a wider garden-care brand.

Continued innovation

Like other successful manufacturers, Flymo on average launch six new products every year to maintain their lead in the market. Since the launch of the first Gardenvac product in March 1993, they have been working on a range of further innovations and the first of these was introduced in summer

Figure C2.3   Flymo Gardenvac Plus. Reproduced by kind permission of Flymo Limited

1995. The only advantage that the traditional US blowervac products had over the original Gardenvac was that, through utilizing the 'dirty fan' principle, they automatically mulched any debris collected. Whilst this meant that twigs and litter blocked the fan and cans could not be picked up at all, it had provided rival manufacturers with a means of compacting leaves and grass, increasing the amount of debris that could be collected within the bag; something which the first Gardenvac could not do. Therefore to provide this additional facility, in November 1993, only eight months after launch, Flymo began working on the inclusion of one of their other areas of core technology into a second generation of the product (Figure C2.3) which was scheduled for release eighteen months later. By incorporating a mono-filament cutting line used in their trimmers at the top of the main tube and driving it from the same motor as the fan, they created a product which not only shredded grass cuttings, leaves and litter, but one which could also allow solid debris such as twigs and cans to pass straight through into the collecting bag. This incremental improvement helped Flymo to maintain their dominance of this sector of the market and was the first of a number of innovations to be introduced over the following years.

Summary

This case history illustrates a number of key issues associated with the development of an innovative product. Primarily it gives a good example of the thought, experimentation and subsequent development that goes into the inception, creation and realization of a new product. It demonstrates some of the difficulties encountered by an individual inventor in finding a manufacturer who is genuinely interested in making the commitment to develop a concept into a marketable and manufacturable product, and also indicates some of the problems associated with successfully licensing a design to such an organization. Finally it highlights the advantages that companies can gain from acquiring a truly innovative product from outside the organization. It shows that, although many commercial risks have to be taken and, to develop the product, significant resources need to be provided, the rewards that stand to be gained from the successful marketing of a well designed product for which there is an identified market opportunity are, particularly in this instance, considerable.

3 Organization for new product development

Introduction

Having a clearly defined product development strategy and an awareness of the contribution of innovation are not the only requirements for successful product development. There is another key component and that is its organization. No matter how clear the project objectives or how innovative the concept, without a well structured company organization within which product development programmes can carefully be planned and the necessary resources provided, the chances of successfully producing a competitive, marketable and manufacturable product are considerably reduced.

Unlike the production, promotion and distribution of existing products, new product development is not a 'steady state' activity. It is rarely routine and there is little repetition. Although two separate programmes may be similar generically, there will frequently be different priorities to be addressed, different product characteristics to be accommodated and different market and technological environments in which to develop and launch the products. New product development is, by its very nature, a cross-disciplinary process and cannot therefore be a segregated functional activity but, to be successful, has to occur with the participation of varied personnel drawn from across the company.

This chapter describes how manufacturers organize their new product development activities and structure the company to support them. It initially examines some of the varied organizational structures that have been adopted by companies and goes on to describe the different approaches to the organization of product development which occurs within these structures. An overview of the traditional sequential approach is followed by an explanation of a parallel approach to working and the benefits that can be achieved through using it effectively. The use of teams both within functions and across disciplines is described, the particular support requirements that are associated with teamwork are detailed and the crucial role of the team leader in focusing effort and driving projects forward is addressed. Project management and the planning, monitoring and control of development programmes are discussed and lastly the demands on the corporate culture to support product development are covered.

Company organization

Manufacturing companies are structured in a number of different ways. Some are formalized with centralized decision making, some are decentralized with devolved responsibility whilst others follow more informal arrangements. The subject of the organization of companies, their structure and the relationships that occur between the various individuals and functions within the organization has been the focus of considerable interest for industrialists and academics for many years. How the organization develops as the company grows, the changing roles of managers, how power is controlled, how people work together and the various differences between Japanese, European and American organizational cultures have all been individually examined at length. However, across all companies there are a number of common structures within which most manufacturers can be considered to fit. Whichever of these is adopted by an individual company can heavily influence how its new product development activity is organized.

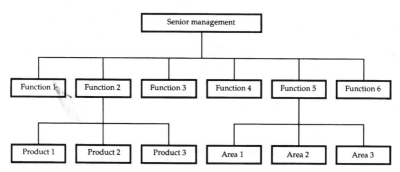

Figure 3.1 Functional company organization

Most common amongst established companies are functionally based organizational structures where senior management directly control a number of separate functions, some of which, such as manufacturing and sales, may be split either into various product groups or geographical areas (Figure 3.1). This type of formal, centralized organization allows for a strong managerial structure with information continually flowing up and down the company to and from senior management. However, although appropriate for some companies, if there are a number of different products involved, this can become multi-layered involving more and more managers and becoming correspondingly inefficient. If large and particularly multinational organizations were structured in this way, decision making would become extremely long-winded and lines of control would be strained. Therefore such manufacturers are often organized in a more decentralized manner. As represented by Figure 3.2, a company such as Electrolux may be split into several separate international areas all with their own functional

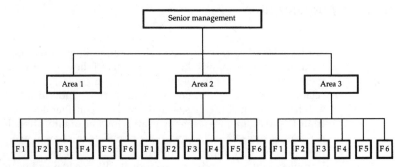

Figure 3.2 Functional company – diversification by area

activities able to design, manufacture and market products in their individual regions. Although there may be cross-over between different areas for the development of common products, assessment of marketing strategies or coordination of finance and the overall organization remains controlled from a central senior management grouping, European products can be developed, manufactured and marketed in Europe and American products can be developed, manufactured and marketed in the USA.

Alternatively a manufacturer operating in one or more sales areas may be structured around different product types, each with its own functional activities (Figure 3.3). These may again share common technology, processes or strategies where appropriate but the overall structure remains formal. Several companies who adopt this approach choose to centralize one or more functions across the whole organization either to improve efficiency or provide common features (Figure 3.4). Sony and Philips both have centralized design activities where the majority of their products are developed thereby allowing for a high level of coordination particularly of industrial design across several product sectors, whilst in Britain, Fujitsu ICL have kept design specific to each of three product divisions, choosing instead to share common manufacturing and sales activities across the company.

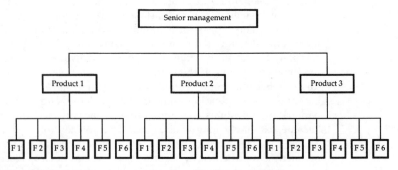

Figure 3.3 Functional company – diversification by product

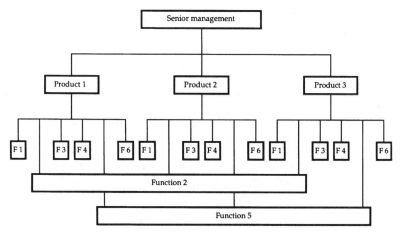

Figure 3.4 Functional company – diversification by product: centralized functions

All of the above formalized structures can be found in some configuration in the majority of established manufacturers. However, in a number of companies, particularly new, small or high technology manufacturers driven by one core technology or an individual entrepreneur, the organization may be more informal (Figure 3.5). Although having identifiable leadership, by enabling direct contact between functions and individuals,

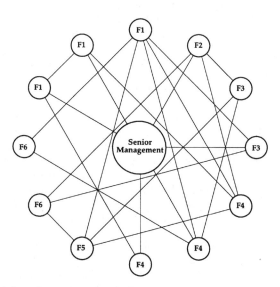

Figure 3.5 Informal company organization

this can allow for quick decision making, shared resources and be particularly beneficial to innovative product development. Through having a less hierarchical approach to the corporate organization as a whole, in many cases the opportunities for new ideas to be generated and discussed are greater in such a structure.

Whilst the overall structure of the organization is therefore largely dependent on the size and age of the company and is driven by the type of products being manufactured, where they are being produced and how and where they are sold, it can clearly be highly influential on product development within the company and how it is itself organized. The way in which the individual functions are coordinated, how resources are managed and the inter-relationships between the relevant areas and personnel within the manufacturer very much sets the organizational parameters within which product development can occur.

Concurrent engineering

Products were traditionally designed, made and sold by independent craftsmen, and all the various activities involved in the development process were usually undertaken by one person. Although the individual designer/ maker would follow no formalized system, a product such as a table, chair or cart would first be designed to fulfil the specified requirements of the user, the appropriate raw materials necessary to manufacture it would be collected or brought and the separate components would be individually made and assembled together. The resulting product would then either be supplied direct to the customer who had ordered it, displayed for sale in the craftsman's studio or taken to market to be sold.

Today the fundamental stages are the same now as they have always been. However, as most products have become more complicated, more people have become involved in their development with different specialists undertaking the varied design, manufacture and marketing roles. As these tasks have become separated into what are now totally different functional responsibilities, there has been a natural tendency for each operation to occur sequentially, one after the other. Rather than one person perhaps identifying the customer's needs, designing the product and simultaneously thinking about how the varied components would be made and put together, the various stages became separated and correspondingly easily isolated. Moreover, as products have in recent years become even more complex, so too has the development process and, in turn, each stage has now been subdivided into a series of component phases.

Not surprisingly, as mass production was introduced and developed throughout the twentieth century, the typical product development process has become a collection of up to twenty individual stages and, to undertake all these, inputs from a whole range of different specialists have become necessary. The 'sequential' approach to product development (Figure 3.6) with each function taking it in turn to take responsibility for a project and

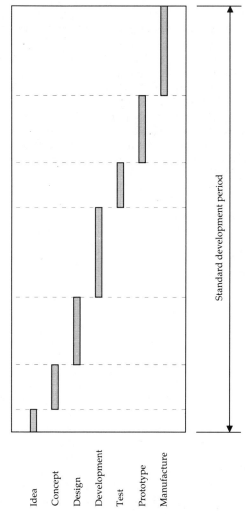

Figure 3.6 Sequential product development

make their contribution before passing it on to the next, became the norm throughout manufacturing. Marketing may identify a new product opportunity, R&D would investigate and develop the technology and generate concepts which would be handed over to design to be turned into manufacturable products. Production engineers would then design and order tooling and plan the production process which would, in turn be undertaken by manufacturing who would supply the end product to sales and marketing for distribution. Although clearly logical and, on the surface, easy to understand and therefore manage, this sequential approach has been gradually found to have several faults.

Whilst individual roles and responsibilities are arguably relatively clear and the transfer between stages allows control of risk, there is little requirement for communication between functions. The only strictly necessary contact occurs whenever a project is passed from one function to the next as it progresses through the development programme, but, by this time, omissions and mistakes have frequently been made. Common problems which occur include: between R&D and design where it may be found that the developed technology was not entirely compatible with the rest of the product; between design and production where it can frequently become apparent that details of the design are either difficult or impossible to manufacture; or between manufacture and marketing were it might be realized that the developed product does not match the original specification. In addition a bottleneck in one stage can slow or even stop the whole process. To overcome these and many other similar misunderstandings, it became standard practice for projects to be passed back and forth between functions at each interface for rethinking, redesign or rework and these inefficiencies built up to both lengthen overall development periods and increase project costs.

As an attempt to address some of these problems, in the early 1980s companies such as Xerox, Canon and NEC introduced a planned period of 'overlap' between consecutive stages (Figure 3.7). Rather than having a point at which the project and responsibility for it was wholly passed from one department to the next, they planned periods around the hand-over date during which the functions involved would work together to identify and resolve any problems with the design, thereby smoothing the transition from one stage to another. In practice, by reducing iteration between stages, this 'sashimi' technique was found to improve the overall flow of the development process in the companies adopting it but, because it only addressed the specific interfaces between consecutive stages, it did not help to solve other problems. Inefficiencies such as the developed product not meeting the original specification, caused by an incremental change of the design during the project, were still possible. In addition, this modification failed to resolve one of the key deficiencies of the sequential approach – the departmental ownership of the project. Since, once a project had been signed off and passed onto the next function, it was no longer the responsibility of the preceding function, as with the sequential approach there was still a common tendency for minor errors to be either hidden or left unresolved.

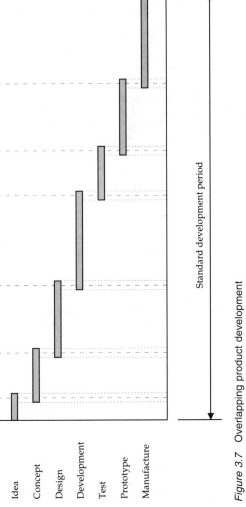

Figure 3.7 Overlapping product development

Furthermore, unlike the traditional craftsman who had complete control of the whole project, because various tasks were still being undertaken by separate functions with only occasional inter-functional communication, there was rarely anyone whose key interest was in both the project and the quality of the developed product rather than the effectiveness of one or two isolated phases of its development.

As a means to overcome these problems, an improved approach to the organization of product development which had been advocated for a number of years was adopted and introduced into a range of manufacturing companies in the late 1980s. Variously termed simultaneous engineering, concurrent engineering or parallel working, this has focused attention on the project as a whole rather than the individual stages. By enabling different operations to be undertaken in parallel (Figure 3.8), not only is the overall development period reduced, but the needs of the project as a whole are better satisfied. Primarily by involving all functions throughout the project from concept to production, all aspects and implications of the design can be addressed as it develops. Through the use of regular reviews throughout the development programme at which all functions are represented, the project can be constantly evaluated and assessed against the varied criteria of each function. For example, by having production engineering and manufacturing involved during concept development and detail design, it can be ensured that the end-product will compliment the production facilities available and can be designed to be easy to both manufacture and assemble. Whilst the major role of R&D personnel is still completed early on in the process, their continued involvement can enable additional technical improvements to be identified and incorporated as the project progresses. By enabling marketing to be party to design decisions, they are able to enhance the information provided within the original brief or specification and, through consultation, can help select the most appropriate options for the customer and the market. Even though this may concern relatively simple issues such as colour, texture or weight, being able to influence the product during the genesis of its design means that the current needs of the market can be better met and no subsequent modifications are required to the developed product before launch.

That said there are limitations to this approach. It requires considerably more effort from individual project members, more effective programme management and there are some projects for which it is considered inappropriate. Specifically large projects such as those in aerospace often demand the more formalized sequential approach to enable their scale to be accommodated and, because it is orientated around collective working from the start, the concurrent approach is often inappropriate for R&D-led high-innovation projects where the early stages require more time and cannot be easily integrated. But, although this approach is not as easily predetermined as the sequential or overlapping options and is therefore more complex to manage, it does enable decisions to be taken based on inputs from all interested parties and therefore more relevant to the needs of the project as a whole rather than to any individual stage or function. However, whilst this

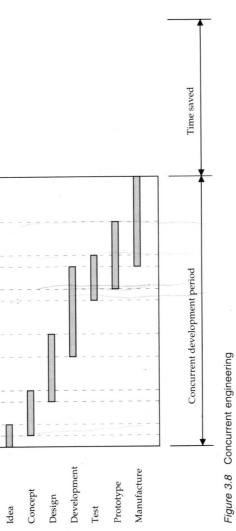

Idea
Concept
Design
Development
Test
Prototype
Manufacture

Concurrent development period

Time saved

Figure 3.8 Concurrent engineering

may appear to be a simple theoretical concept, in practice successfully undertaking concurrent engineering within product development requires not only a change in corporate philosophy but also a fundamental modification in organization. Although the sequential approach developed in tandem with the growth of separated functional departments to undertake the respective stages, the concurrent approach has been found to work best when used in partnership with interdisciplinary project teams.

Teams

The fundamental concept of teams is nothing new. In the military, using groups of soldiers collectively to carry out specific tactical operations has been in existence since Roman times. In sport having between five and fifteen individuals all working together as one effective unit has been the foundation of games the world over for thousands of years. Similarly, in manufacturing, the use of a team of designers as the core of development projects has been commonplace in large projects for many years. However the principle of having multi-disciplinary or cross-functional teams made up of a selection of individual specialists has not, until recently, been a regular occurrence within industry. Elsewhere, in areas such as medicine where an operating theatre team frequently includes not only the surgeon and an assistant but also an anaesthetist and assistant, a theatre nurse and orderlies supported by technicians and radiographers, multi-disciplinary teams have been in use for some time. In product development, the concept has only really occurred in parallel with the adoption of the principles of concurrent engineering. If, as indicated above, the whole project and not one or two individual stages or functional activities is to be the main focus of attention, having a group of individuals whose key interests are in the project and the product which is developed is a major advantage to any programme. By having primary allegiance from designers, production engineers, marketing personnel, etc., to the team, the project and its successful progression from concept to manufacture rather than to their respective departments, the results in both the effectiveness of the overall programme and the quality of the developed product are frequently highly significant.

The key benefits which are available from the use of multi-functional teams include issues such as:

- By eliminating iteration between functions because they are all working together on the same project, development periods can be reduced.
- By overcoming hierarchical structures within organizations, decision making can become decentralized to the project and the decisions taken are more appropriate to it.
- Because the focus of the team members is on the project, the relevant information is more effectively filtered from the mass of market statistics, technical data and manufacturing figures present within departments and outside.

- By having a collective objective and project goals, traditional problems associated with division of labour are overcome.
- By exchanging ideas on a continual basis, both individuals' and the team's knowledge and learning is increased.

Team organization

Associated with the use of teams there are a number of issues which manufacturers have to address concerning selection of the team members, the role of the project leader and the supply of support resources. But, above this, how a team actually fits within the overall company organizational structure has to first be determined and this can be significantly affected by company size and which overall company structure is in place.

In small companies where perhaps only a couple of development projects are being undertaken at one time, the creation of a full-time project team may not be practicable. In this instance it is often more appropriate to have say one designer permanently associated with each project and other team members from marketing, production, finance or quality involved on a part-time basis. Having other responsibilities associated with the 'solid state' activities of manufacturing and selling existing product, there is frequently insufficient staff resources for personnel from these functions to be permanently integrated within the product development team on a full-time basis. Instead, being part of the project team is just one of their roles and, although this may not be ideal, by ensuring that the project is managed effectively, that all are able to contribute where and when they are required and by recognizing the purpose and relative importance of the development activity, the benefits of the team approach can still be achieved.

In larger companies, where several projects may be in progress at the same time and there are usually sufficient resources for more personnel to be wholly concerned with a development project, there are a number of alternative options for the organization of development teams. Most commonly there will, as discussed earlier, be a formalized functional organization in place with the various disciplines either co-located or split by region. In this situation companies often adopt a matrix structure (Figure 3.9) were team members from an appropriate selection of functional backgrounds work together on the project and individually draw upon resources and support from their 'parent' departments. This allows the majority of functional resources to remain centralized whilst not restricting the activity and effectiveness of the individual teams which can either be integrated through departments or operate independently of each other. This can be effective in, amongst others, companies where several similar products are being developed in parallel.

Alternatively separate development teams may each have their own dedicated support team who draw on collective resources both from within the company and from outside (Figure 3.10). By partially decentralizing resources away from departments, this option can free the individual team members from a number of the secondary responsibilities such as

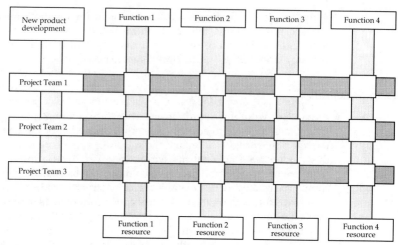

Figure 3.9 Matrix team organization

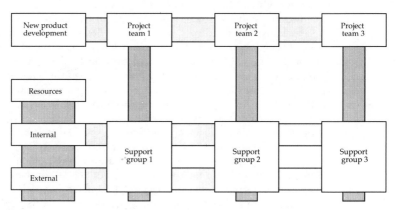

Figure 3.10 Team organization – dedicated support groups

identifying components, obtaining background market information or materials data, and enable them to concentrate on the core product development activity. This approach can be used to great effect in companies where projects being undertaken concern the development of a number of different products which share similar technology, address similar markets or can use common manufacturing facilities as illustrated in the accompanying case study of the development of Mouseman Sensa by Logitech. This is therefore also common in companies with product diversified organizations with centralized design activities shown in Figure 3.4.

A third alternative is to further decentralize the organization and adopt a more organic approach. Figure 3.11 illustrates an open system where individual project teams draw upon independent support resources which, rather than being centralized within departments, are selected and coordinated by the teams themselves. Although potentially increasing the core team's workload, this option allows for closer contact between the team and component suppliers, subcontractors and external information sources. It is particularly appropriate in the less formalized organizations and function based companies where several totally different projects with little in common are being undertaken.

It is therefore evident that in a contemporary development programme, the choice of approach between sequential and concurrent is both influenced by and, in turn, can influence the overall company structure. If products are to be developed in the traditional manner the inter-relationship between functions is not so critical but when multi-disciplinary teams are used, how

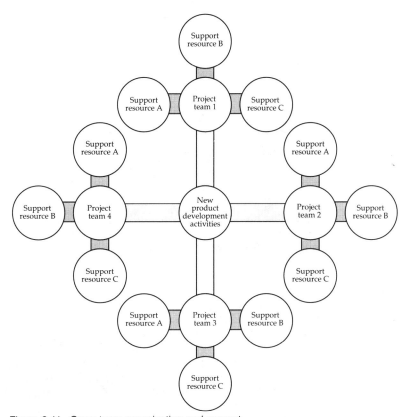

Figure 3.11 Open team organization and support

they are organized and supported and from where they are resourced is dependent either on effective departmental management of resources across several project teams or on having dedicated cross-functional resources made available to each team.

Team creation

Whichever of these varied organizational structures is adopted, there are a number of issues which are common to all multi-disciplinary teams and have become critical to their effectiveness. Foremost is the creation of the team itself and the selection of the individual team members. Whilst in small companies there may be little option of which personnel to involve with selection being primarily dictated by availability, in larger organizations where more choice is available, selecting the right people can be pivotal to the success of a project. Clearly, there is a need to have a group of people working together with the required representation of the various skills necessary for the project to be undertaken, but these individuals also have to be selected to fulfil additional criteria: team members need to be able to work together, share ideas, discuss alternatives and be willing to accept team decisions. Development teams are no place for loners who single mindedly pursue their own inclinations with little consideration for others' opinions. Team members have to be committed to both the project and the team, to be willing to give 110 per cent when necessary and to be able to adapt the the changing needs of the project as it progresses. Team members have to be good communicators. They need to be capable of clearly expressing their ideas and opinions, of listening to others and able to discuss, negotiate and accept compromise. Although a particular decision may not be felt to be the optimum choice from one function's perspective, if overall it is the most appropriate to the project, all have to be willing to accept it and work with it. Finally, the team frequently works best if there is an evident team spirit which not only serves partially to drive the project and motivate but also unites the individual team members so that they feel that they belong to the project and own it. Whilst some companies go so far as to provide team sweatshirts and arrange social events to give the team a visible identity and cement the relationships, others achieve the same effect by fostering the team culture in more subtle but no less effective ways.

In terms of size, the number of personnel selected as members of the team can vary considerably. Sometimes there may be a core team of only three or four, supported by a similar number of others, while in some cases, most commonly on large projects such as the development of a totally new car or computer system, teams of over 100 are not unknown. However, in these situations, the overall team is frequently broken down into smaller sub-groups which each address individual details of the design and are centrally coordinated to ensure overall coherence and compatibility. Although there are no hard and fast rules regarding how large or small a team should be, it appears that core teams of between five and twelve, supported by up to twenty additional personnel, are the most common in product development today. This mirrors the size of teams in other areas such as sport and medicine and allows for effective sharing of workload within an effective unit.

Although teams are frequently created afresh on a project-by-project basis, in some cases, most notably in Japanese organizations, there is a growing tendency to maintain continuity of team membership from one project to the next. By having a team designing a new mobile phone who have already developed a number of earlier models and are therefore aware of potential problems, companies like Matsushita feel that the effectiveness and performance of the team and hence the quality of the product can be continuously improved. By contrast, in many European organizations it is more common to disband the team once the project is completed and, for the next programme, choose a different combination of personnel, some from the first project and some new. The advantages claimed for this approach include greater flexibility, an ability to rotate personnel around, thus enabling 'best practice' to be disseminated with individuals through transfer of learning by 'osmosis' and the prevention of errors occurring from careless assumptions made due to over-familiarity.

As for functional representation, most teams in some capacity, involve personnel from marketing, R&D, design, production engineering and manufacturing and more and more often, sales, quality and finance supported by market research, purchasing and senior management. In addition many companies also involve representatives of external organizations either within the core team itself or as part of the support structure. Marketing and design consultants are commonly integrated within the core team, often playing a key role in the direction and development of the project. By drawing from their specialist knowledge of market forces, current trends, user expectations and areas of technical expertise, they are used to provide vital guidance within the team and help to ensure that the developed product is appropriate to the market and the technology. Although not always as knowledgeable about the specific product and its market as in-house personnel, such consultants can use their experiences from developing and marketing products in different sectors or with other companies to apply ideas and techniques which benefit the product, improving its design, decreasing its cost or changing its image.

Particularly in larger projects such as the development of a new car, companies like Toyota and Honda have pioneered a movement away from issuing drawings from which component suppliers manufacture the applicable parts, towards involving these suppliers in the design of not only these components but, in some cases, also in influencing the overall assembly. Rather than giving them a set of drawings and specifications of radio cassette players for the Xantia, Citroen brought Bosch engineers into the design team to help develop a better integrated in-car entertainment system with controls within and around the steering wheel operating the radio, cassette and CD player embedded within the facia. In addition, many of today's leading manufacturers also involve toolmakers and other sub-contractors in the development team to help determine what specific design details would, for example, make a moulding cheaper, increase its rigidity or improve its appearance. By having this direct input from external organizations who know most about their specialist areas, manufacturers find that the overall efficiency of both the team and the developed product is improved significantly.

Project team leader

With such a variety of different personnel within both the core and support teams, the role of the project leader in enabling the team to achieve its objectives and maintaining continuity and coherence throughout the programme can be considered as another critical component which contributes to a successful project. Whether undertaken by a number of separate departments or by a multi-disciplinary team, all projects have a project leader on whose shoulders lies the responsibility for the completion of the programme.

In some companies the project leader monitors progress as part of senior management, in others he is integrated within the core team whilst in others he is often drawn from one of the key functions involved. No matter from which functional background he may originate, it is the role of the project leader to ensure that the project progresses smoothly, meeting all interim objectives and targets on time and within budget, to make sure that the necessary resources are available when and where they are required and to also act as the primary channel of communication between the project team, senior management and any external organizations involved. Whilst in some companies the role is conducted in a supervisory context, in others, such as described in Case studies 3 (Logitech) and 4 (Polaroid), it has become very much of a hands-on position. When the project is initiated it is the project leader who helps to select the appropriate personnel and who checks that the schedule is realistic and can be met; during the development programme it is the project leader who keeps not only himself but also all members of the team and senior management informed of progress, who encourages all involved and helps the inevitable difficulties which arise to be overcome; and, towards the end of the programme, it is the project leader who makes sure that everything comes together at the right time so that production can be initiated and product launch can occur as planned.

Many companies choose to nominate project leaders from functional backgrounds appropriate to the project whilst others prefer to use specialist project leaders who have no functional bias but are trained and experienced in planning and organization, can communicate effectively with all involved and are sufficiently aware of all the contributing issues to ensure that they are all addressed as the project progresses. For some innovation based companies this latter option may be inappropriate because technical skills can be more important than administrative capabilities and a project leader is needed with specialist knowledge available from only R&D or design. However, with the rise of project management as an identifiable profession in its own right, it is likely that in the majority of companies developing incrementally improved products there will continue to be a growth in the use of dedicated personnel for this role.

Whatever the background, it is the project leader who is the essential driving force behind a development programme. He has overall responsibility for the project meeting target dates and objectives and to do this has to have a clear understanding of the project goals. The project team leader is the person who not only has to motivate the team, ensuring that all the individual roles are undertaken with the required resources available, but also needs to maintain senior management support. To achieve this it is becoming more and more common for such leaders to have both the freedom and autonomy to not only select the team and determine individual roles and responsibilities, but also to take the key decisions and set the project goals, budgets and schedules which all form part of the overall project management.

Project management

Irrespective of which approach to the organization of product development activities is taken, the project itself has to be well planned, managed and controlled. Only by carefully setting achievable targets and realistic interim objectives and scheduling a development programme according to its specific needs can the necessary budgets be defined and resource requirements identified and made available at the appropriate time. It is frequently the responsibility of the team leader to undertake this either independently or in some cases with the support of programme managers.

Foremost the project goals have to be determined. These are the key objectives for which projects are undertaken and the parameters against which they are evaluated. They not only involve overall aims in terms of the end product being developed, but they also consider interim stages within the programme. The brief or specification is clearly a key driver of these and is becoming identified as being more and more important within all development activities. It communicates to the development team exactly what it is that they are required to design, develop and manufacture. It can detail target markets, prices and customers, product features, specific technology to be incorporated, manufacturing processes to be used and production levels to be achieved as well as numerous other supporting information. In doing this, it has to be clear to all involved and it is therefore of little benefit if, for example, it is written by marketing without consultation with designers and manufacturing or if the development team are unable to comment on it, provide feedback and arrive at an agreed description of the proposed product which is acceptable to all. Some companies tend to treat this document, the briefing session and other associated meetings which take place right at the start of a project too lightly. However, it is here where, without clear and concise instructions, projects can very quickly veer away from their intended paths or critical omissions can be made. It is therefore in the interests of all parties involved to ensure that it is treated with the necessary care and attention to detail and is developed in close consultation. From this, realistic interim targets and deliverables for specific stages such as dates for data release, sampling and production start-up can be determined through discussion and the development programme itself can be planned around these points.

Although because of having more distinct start and finish points for individual stages, planning a sequentially organized programme can be less difficult than a concurrent project, both require team leaders and pro-gramme managers to assess accurately how long each phase of the development is likely to take, who is to undertake them and what equipment and funding may be required. Many products today are complex and consequently so too are the development processes through which they are created. Therefore all the key stages need to be both individually planned in detail and scheduled to fit the overall programme appropriately. Whereas with sequential development it is possible to determine a clear critical path within the project around which the overall schedule can be built, with the concurrent approach such an option is not available. As so many stages overlap and key decisions in one can affect all the rest, it is rarely possible to identify one specific critical path but, instead, there are a whole series of potential scenarios to be accommodated. A two-week delay in design development could cause testing to be held up thus altering the start date of manufacture and consequently causing product launch to be delayed by a month or so. It is therefore necessary for companies adopting the team approach to plan their project schedules not only to minimize the development period but also to be sufficiently adaptable and flexible to cope with a range of potentially different outcomes. Without establishing these basic parameters, an overall schedule cannot be produced and, only by using this detailed level of planning, can development projects able to meet the required project goals be undertaken successfully without delays.

Because of the variability in the length of the pre-development stages associated with business planning, R&D and market research, most companies tend to only schedule the concept to production phases of the development programme in detail as these are the stages where the majority of project funds are committed. Studies (Berliner and Brimson, 1988) have determined that it is during these stages that the decisions concerning between 70 and 90 per cent of the total project costs involved in manufacturing a new product are taken, thereby making these a major area of concern for most companies. With accurate estimates of the length of individual phases, the overall schedule can be created as a composite representation of the varied activities to be undertaken and enables the key points in the programme to be identified and the associated requirements for the project at these points to be determined. In many projects individual resource requirements can be substantial and their availability needs to be planned well in advance of use. Items such as bolsters for tooling, prototype packaging and text for manuals and brochures all have to be commissioned, ordered or written months ahead so that, when they are required, they are to hand and prepared to the necessary level ensuring that no delay to the project as a whole will occur.

To monitor and evaluate the progress of a project throughout the development programme, many organizations use regular formal meetings, commonly termed stage gates or phase reviews interspersed with informal discussions. By having predetermined dates when senior management, project leaders and representatives from all functions involved will collectively assess how well a project is progressing and what goals have been achieved, any weaknesses can be quickly identified and action taken to address them. By determining what has to be undertaken during each phase and the stage at which it should be at the time of the phase review, both managers and project teams can ensure that all business, market, design and manufacture requirements are met and that no one area is allowed to drag. In addition, by linking control of funding to the project passing such phase reviews, some companies choose to ensure that all requirements are met before progression.

In 1992, GPT, the British telecommunications manufacturer, adopted a nine-stage phase review process for use in its new product development programmes. Building on traditional techniques of monitoring sequential projects, this system – for use in concurrent programmes – developed a set of goals across all functions at each stage. Figure 3.12 shows a typical GPT development programme divided into individual stages and illustrates the progression of individual plans and tasks throughout the project. Phase reviews occur at the end of each stage and allow progress against agreed project goals to be monitored. At each review 'deliverables' are assessed by a panel drawn from senior management and the project team. Independent assessors from within the organization or consultants who are able to judge the deliverables objectively identify any deficiencies that may exist and determine actions to be taken before the project can pass the review.

Although in each project, the goals and therefore the deliverables may be slightly different, typical deliverables for Phase 2 'Feasibility' are:

- marketing plan
- market requirements specification
- outline systems and product specifications
- business case/new product investment application
- project management plan
- outline engineering plan
- outline manufacturing and procurement plan
- outline consumer services plan
- outline test and verification plan
- regulatory approvals
- risk analysis

In consultation with a chairperson and programme managers, it is decided if the deliverables are all at the required stage of development, whether or not the review has therefore been passed and if the project can progress to the next

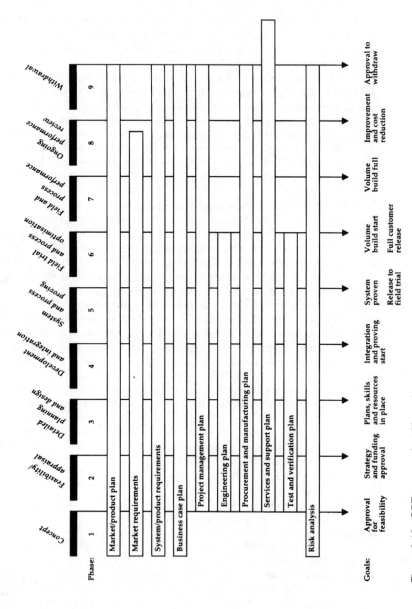

Figure 3.12 GPT new product life-cycle

stage. If only minor actions are required to overcome deficiencies, the project is allowed to progress, conditional upon these being completed within thirty days; however, if there are major problems the review is failed. In the case of a first time fail, further investment is withheld. For a conditional fail, action is recommended to overcome the deficiencies with a rerun of the review thirty days later. If after this second review the result is still a fail then the project is reviewed with directors with a view to cancelling it.

This type of system enables the whole process to be evaluated on a regular basis and kept on track. In addition, at each stage confirmation of quality execution of tasks can be obtained. If undertaken efficiently it thereby allows companies to control both projects and their finance accordingly. However, although now common place in many manufacturers, such systems are by no means perfect and for true concurrent programmes contain a number of flaws (Cooper, 1994). Because an entire project can be put on hold while one or two deficient tasks are completed, unnecessary and expensive delays in other tasks can occur; in contemporary concurrent projects there are often significant overlaps between stages, with one starting before the previous one is completed. All projects have to go through every review which, although appropriate for most large programmes, can hamper smaller low risk projects which may benefit from taking opportune short cuts to save time; and, having a rigidly documented system can lead to unnecessary detail which shifts focus away from innovation towards ensuring that the project merely jumps through the prescribed hoops.

To overcome these deficiencies, companies such as Procter & Gamble have developed the system to be more flexible. Rather than having discrete 'stop/ go' decisions, reviews in these organizations favour more 'conditional go' options enabling non-problematic tasks to continue while attention and resources are applied to the identified problems to make up lost time. As detailed in Chapter 4, addressing rapid product development, this has several advantages in terms of increased speed and reduced time to market but is also higher risk. Decisions can be taken on minimal information and can therefore be more dependent on educated guesswork, experience and instinct. Consequently more responsibility is also placed on team members to achieve their roles and on the project leader to ensure that all the various tasks do come together as planned.

Culture and climate

Industrial commentators, politicians and consultants frequently talk of the need for innovation culture within organizations, but, when applied to product development the demand is not only for an environment in which new ideas can be generated, but for one in which these ideas can also receive support and be integrated into well planned efficient development programmes. 3M is often cited as an organization in which innovation is encouraged and, through generous internal funding, assisted by research and development. However, whilst offering an excellent example in this context, for manufacturers addressing immediate needs of product development, Hewlett Packard, Matsushita and Toyota may be companies to emulate. As well as using innovation as an integral part of their new product development activities, because of the complexity of their products, they frequently establish a wider development culture.

From the preceding overview of organizational structures and approaches to product development and its management, it is evident that to enable multi-disciplinary teams to operate successfully within an organization, an environment and culture supportive of their needs has to be put in place. To a degree, it is easier for product development to occur within a flexible organic organization where growth is primarily dependent on new products for new markets than in the more established formalized manufacturers. Naturally having greater functional integration can enable some small companies to react quickly to changing conditions and position themselves and their products accordingly. On the other hand, large manufacturers usually have greater resources at their disposal and, although sometimes slower to respond and adapt to the same influences, due to having an established product range with existing market share, they can use their technology and knowledge to great effect.

However, across all types of forward looking manufacturing organizations there is a growing dependency on new product development and increasing recognition of its contribution to growth. This is being acknowledged not only by designers and senior management but also by manufacturing and marketing personnel. Consequently the status of new product development activities within companies is increasing and the corresponding need to support it is becoming more frequently acknowledged. For some manufacturers, establishing product development teams within their existing structure is feasible and commonplace, but in others it is not so simple. The change from a traditional to contemporary approach to product development is, like the use of new technology, not just an overnight switch. Change takes time, causes disruption and shifts focus and hence for companies choosing to improve their development activities, adapting even their organizational structure to one more appropriate to the needs of product development can often be required.

A change in the way projects are organized can bring with it modification of functional relationships, relocation of personnel, alteration of production facilities and sometimes even a revision of the way the company does business. The importance of having well-resourced development teams has been mentioned earlier but the support required for product development to occur successfully can include more than the provision of funding and availability of equipment. A reduction in bureaucracy and the creation of a 'can-do' culture is also necessary. Whilst the management of any task inevitably involves meetings, reports and other paperwork, companies such as Logitech have sought to reduce this to a minimum and rearrange tasks to enable team members to focus on their core roles. Using new technology, rationalizing management and establishing improved communication systems can all play an important part in assisting a project's progress.

Chapter summary

This chapter has given an indication of some of the many issues which contribute to the organization and management of new product development activities. It has identified the key organizational structures used by manufacturers and has discussed alternative approaches to the organization of new product development which occur within these. The characteristics of sequential, overlapping and concurrent product development have been detailed and the advantages of using teams, particularly of a multi-functional nature have been outlined. Within this area, the specific role of the project team leader has been addressed and an introduction to some of the issues associated with project management have been identified. Lastly the importance of achieving and maintaining an appropriate culture to support product development has been touched upon. The key issues addressed can be summarized as:

- Whilst some companies are informally organized, others follow formal structures which can be grouped by area, product or functional activity.
- Manufacturers' overall organizational structure influence how their new product development activities are themselves organized.
- Traditionally products have been developed sequentially with one activity following on from another.
- To increase their effectiveness, many companies now try to follow the concurrent approach to product development with a number of activities occurring simultaneously.
- Forming teams, particularly multi-functional teams, is seen as the most beneficial means of successfully enabling concurrent product development to take place.
- The project team leader has a critical role in ensuring that a team functions effectively with minimal interference but sufficient support.
- Clear project goals and regular project reviews are seen as two effective means of managing new product development programmes.
- To enhance the effectiveness of product development activities, a supportive culture is extremely beneficial but often requires change to both the structure and the environment.

References

Barczak, G. and Wilemon, D. (1992) Successful New Product Team Leaders. *Industrial Marketing Management*, **21**, 61–68.

Berliner, C. and Brimson, J.A. (eds) (1988) *Cost Management for Today's Advanced Manufacturing: The CAM-I Conceptual Design*. Harvard Business School Press.

Cooper, R.G. (1994) Third-Generation New Product Processes. *Journal of Product Innovation Management*, **11**, 3–14.

Handy, C. (1993) *Understanding Organisations*. Penguin.

PA Consulting Group (1993) *Manufacturing into the Late 1990s*. HMSO.

Takeuchi, H. and Nonaka, I. (1986) The New New Product Development Game. *Harvard Business Review*, **1**, 137–146.

Case study 3: Logitech Mouseman Sensa

Logitech is a multinational manufacturer of computer equipment of which mice are the primary products. The company was founded in Switzerland in 1982 to design, manufacture and market interface equipment for the fast developing computer industry, and over the next decade grew significantly, moving its corporate headquarters to Fremont, California but keeping Switzerland as its financial base. Logitech became the major supplier of mice to most of the world's computer companies including IBM, Compaq, HP and Digital and in the mid-1980s also began to market products direct to retail under its own name. It now operates internationally and has manufacturing facilities in Taiwan, China and Ireland with design occurring in the USA, Ireland and Taiwan and marketing being run regionally: Europe from Switzerland, the Far East from Taiwan and the US from California. There is a very strong focus within the company on product development with 7 per cent of turnover typically being invested directly into new products resulting in twenty-five new products being developed in 1993/94 alone.

The company initially opened its facility in Cork, Ireland, in 1988 primarily as an original equipment manufacturer (OEM) support centre for Apple Computers who had earlier located their European manufacturing operations in the same area. Over the next few years Logitech Ireland grew from being a production facility for US originated products to become a centre for product development in its own right, launching its first mouse in 1991 and subsequently developing a further twelve products during the next three years.

In 1990 Microsoft began to operate in this product sector and subsequently released a number of mouse products to compete with Logitech, particularly in the medium and high end of the retail business. Whilst Logitech had released the successful Mouseman product in 1991 and updated it in 1993, by 1994 Microsoft were known to be preparing another new model for launch the following year and it was clear that, to continue as a major player in the field, Logitech had to develop a new innovative product which would once again take them into the lead.

In September 1994 Logitech therefore launched Mouseman 2, a new mouse developed to maintain the company's share of the high end retail market which at one point had stood at 40 per cent. This product was developed by an international team of engineers, designers, consultants and marketing personnel from the US, Italy and Ireland in a period of less than a year from concept to production. By the end of 1994 Logitech Ireland were manufacturing 140,000 units of the Mouseman 2 product range each month to satisfy the growing market demand.

This case history describes the development of the Mouseman 2 range, focusing in particular on the organizational issues involved. It addresses the changes which took place in their approach to product development, details the creation of the team and the support and resources made available to it and discusses the role of the core team leader, emphasizing how he was a key component, responsible for ensuring that the product was developed successfully.

Background

The manufacture of equipment for the computer industry is divided into two distinct categories; standard products manufactured for branding by the major computer companies and usually higher specification products produced for retail under the manufacturers' own name and sold direct to the consumer. For organizations such as Logitech, the OEM market, supplying mice to companies such as Apple, IBM and Compaq, forms a very high volume but low margin sector whereas the retail business provides greater profit margins and is therefore one in which they have wished to increase their market share.

In 1991 when their main competitor, Microsoft, was beginning to dominate the medium and high end of this retail business, Logitech successfully launched the Mouseman, a new mouse which was specifically designed to compete in this area of the market. Outside the use of more advanced electronics, functionally this product was very similar to other mice so the company tried to push the use of the ergonomic aspects of its shape and emphasize the quality of its design and manufacture. This was a considerable success but in response Microsoft began to make improvements to their product range and therefore, in late 1992, Logitech correspondingly improved the Mouseman, adding weight, incorporating finger indentations for more comfort and a soft cable to give it a higher image. Although this maintained sales for the next year or so this tweaking of the design was essentially only a stop-gap measure and a new product that appealed more directly to users of computer equipment was clearly required. In addition, due to growing competition in the retail side of the business, the company wanted a product which would not only stand out and be markedly different from other mice but which would also achieve this without alienating traditional, perhaps more conservative purchasers of a Mouseman type product.

The new product would also be called Mouseman to both build upon the existing reputation of the original Mouseman but would be available in two variations, Classic and Sensa, to indicate that it was an improved and updated product. However, before it could be designed in detail, the company had to research the various options which were available. Having initiated the original trend in the late 1980s, they were well aware that changing the shape of the product alone was no longer a sufficient innovation for the market: Logitech and their competitors had, over recent years, developed a number of different forms driven from an ergonomic perspective and, to a certain extent, consumers now expected their mice to feel comfortable in the hand, to have buttons positioned in the optimal locations and to also have both a smooth action and a quick response. They therefore had to find something new and resolved to investigate the possibility of introducing a product with a range of different colours, patterns and textures and, to advise them on this, they decided to involve a consultant from the Italian design institute, the Domus Academy. This organization had much experience in advising companies on many aspects of product design to help them accurately to position their products in the market, particularly at the high end. It was felt that they would therefore be the most appropriate people to advise Logitech on what specific combinations of colour, texture and pattern would suit both the product and the market and to recommend how they could be best incorporated within a product which had to be manufactured for a similar price as the competition. Thus the Sensa concept was born.

However, even though Logitech had led the use of shape as a key product differential, they still had to select or create one that would be most appropriate for a major new product. They had launched a number of mice with different external forms over the previous three years, some of which had been more successful than others, and had found that, like conventional ink pens, mice are brought not just on performance but also on how they look and how they feel in the hand, so they too have to be attractive and comfortable to use for extended periods. One recently introduced shape which had received much critical acclaim had been developed for a cordless version of the Mouseman product. Although, mainly because of its cost, this product had not sold in large numbers, regular users and reviewers had all praised its ergonomically led design which had incorporated a number of details such as a backward tapering upper moulding which fitted snugly in the hand. It was therefore decided that the new product would be largely based on the same overall proportions and shape as this cordless model.

As the Mouseman Sensa was to be aimed at both the mid range and high end of the market, a strategic decision was taken to produce it in two distinct versions, a basic model, in the Logitech standard grey for the traditional middle market customers, and, for the more adventurous higher end, premium models in whatever colour, texture, pattern combinations came out of the development programme. As Logitech knew the mid-range market very well from its previous products, it was felt that no extensive market research was necessary for the basic 'Classic' model but, to assess the suggestions from the Domus Academy it was clear that, for the premium 'Sensa' products, a significant market research and testing programme would be required.

Hence, by November 1993, Logitech had decided that they wanted to launch a new product into two sectors. Both versions would share the same technology and would be designed to utilize the same mouldings which were to be based on the Mouseman Cordless, but the models would differ in colour, texture and pattern. Since their main rivals, Microsoft, were expected to introduce a new product, the J-Mouse, around July 1994, Mouseman Classic and Sensa would ideally be launched either just before or at the same time. The 'pointing device' business unit manager, a company vice-president, therefore approved the project and Logitech's board subsequently sanctioned the development of the products to proceed.

Traditional approach

Logitech had been using team based systems for a number of years but, until this project, had always adopted a standard approach to the organization of product development activities typical of most manufacturers in the computer sector. Once approval for a development programme was given, a team would be put together, usually under the leadership of a senior manager who was sometimes given remission to run a project but, more commonly, took it on as an additional role to his other responsibilities. The team would be made up of individuals representing the necessary functional activities which were spread throughout the organization and often throughout the world. Although being part of a development team was a major role, team members would often be involved in other activities related to their discipline and would occasionally also be part of other teams working on different development projects. This led to considerable resource problems such as team members undertaking several different design tasks at the same time and not being kept up to date on the project, its needs and their expected involvement. Furthermore, in such situations team leaders had often found it difficult to keep on top of the project.

New product development projects had, in the past, also been largely driven by marketing who, understandably, always wanted as early a launch date as possible. Consequently they would stipulate what was required by when and all other development activities were reverse scheduled backwards from these predetermined dates. Since marketing usually consulted other functions before setting these targets, some projects would progress as planned. However, although people would always try their best to achieve the targets, more often there would be a series of delays which would build up over the programme, resulting in the launch being postponed. As they were constantly under pressure to deliver on time, problems would arise primarily because individual team members would often draw up schedules based on a list of minimums which could rarely be achieved. Any unforeseen problem, slight delay or minor iteration within the process would therefore affect the whole project and, as marketing rarely understood the detail of the problems, such a delay would lead to either more pressure to meet unrealistic targets or a complete revision of project schedules. Moreover, this approach often resulted in a significant demand on programme managers who, in Logitech, were responsible for pulling all the individual schedules together to ensure that they could all be integrated as required. However they did this with no responsibility for the individual schedules and, because of their position within the company hierarchy, had little authority to impose completion dates. In addition, they frequently had no substantial knowledge of the product development process itself and therefore found it difficult to identify the subtle changes in scheduling of say tooling, prototyping and testing which might have resulted in enabling earlier delivery dates to be achieved.

New approach

However, for the Mouseman Classic/Sensa project a number of key changes were introduced to overcome these problems and reduce the possibility of unforeseen delay. Throughout the company a new approach to product development focused around the concept of a product availability date (PAD). This was defined as the date at which half the first month's worldwide requirement for a new product would be manufactured and in stock ready for supply to retailers. It was initiated partly to overcome a reputation that had grown within the computer industry for manufacturers to advertise a product months earlier than the realistic availability date, but also resulted in a number of significant changes within the company's development process itself. Basically, once a 'PAD' date had been agreed to, it could not be changed and therefore the onus to deliver on time fell on the shoulders of every team member. Late launch was no longer an available option. Project schedules were not based on idealistic minimums but were to be better planned, able to accommodate minor delays and were to be virtually guaranteed to be met. Individual team members now had the authority to say how long tasks would take and, once agreed, no one could force them to complete them in less time. Although this made the overall planned project schedule slightly longer than before, because no delay was acceptable, its successful implementation would, in theory, result in an actual schedule possibly shorter than was usually achieved.

Core team leader

The second major innovation for Logitech in this project was in the selection and role of the core team leader. Rather than having a senior manger seconded onto the project as a part-time job, it was decided to offer a full-time position to a programme coordinator who had extensive experience of product development in industry and had recently successfully managed a smaller project within the company. Since the project was innovative mainly from a marketing rather than technology perspective, they also broke the mould by appointing a non-engineer. Furthermore, not only was this the first time that there had been a core team leader who was not from a technical background, but the opportunity was also given for him to have more personal responsibility than had happened with any previous projects. Whereas the PAD concept gave authority for individual roles to team members by default, the team leader had to take authority for the whole project and with it the main responsibility for its successful completion. For the first time in the company, rather than asking senior managers for resources, the core team leader was, for instance, able to object to insufficient funding or insist on extra support for any inexperienced members of the team. By taking responsibility in this way, he was not only able to delegate tasks to all team members more effectively but, at the same time, also protect them from any distractions from outside. If for example, marketing wanted to change a detail of the product, the core team leader would consult the relevant personnel and only authorize the change if he felt it was appropriate, beneficial to the project and would not cause delay. Whilst this might potentially cause conflict between the team leader and others outside the team, no disturbance would occur within the project.

Resources

The third key change initiated for this project concerned the availability of resources. For the development of Mouseman 2, not only would the core team leader be involved virtually full time, but a number of other key team members would also be able to work continuously on the project. This would be particularly relevant to the mechanical design engineer who, besides being put on the project full time and provided with a support draughtsman when necessary, also had his non-project roles reallocated to others. In addition, the tasks usually undertaken by such a designer in a project were dissected and all the non-design activities were resourced separately by the functional manager to ensure that 100 per cent of the designer's time was available for the design of the product. To further support this approach it was also decided that, wherever possible, the core team should be formed from personnel from one location, namely Logitech Ireland. It was argued that this would minimize resource problems because the majority of the team would be available on hand and more effective intra-team working relationships would also be possible.

Introducing all three of these modifications to their process on one project was therefore a radical move by Logitech but, if undertaken together, they believed that they would provide a framework upon which a successful development programme could be built.

Team creation

The core team leader for the project was appointed at the end of December 1993 and, after flying over to the USA to review the strategy for the product with marketing personnel, in January 1994 he set about creating a worldwide project team (Figure C3.1). Within the project there were to be two streams of activity, termed by Logitech as eight-level and nine-level. The eight-level activities related to the undertaking and completion of the development of the 'hardware' of the product and ensuring that it was successfully transferred into production, whilst the nine-level activities concerned the development of the 'software'; the packaging, the manuals, promotion material and the driving computer software. As marketing were based in the USA it was decided from the start that they would coordinate the nine-level software activities and review with the core team leader on a weekly basis. Since packaging, manuals and software were virtually standardized across the company's products and their development would only involve marketing, a

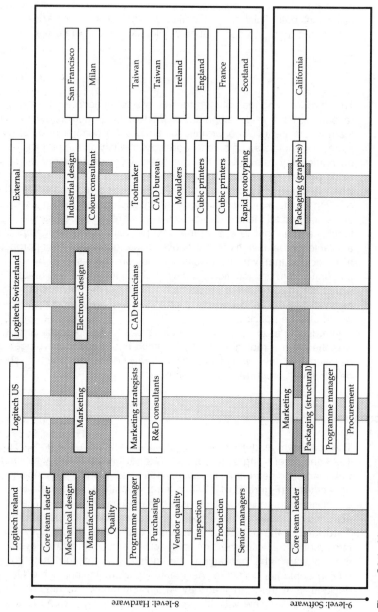

Figure C3.1 Mouseman Sensa project team

packaging designer and a local packaging graphics consultant, all supported by a programme manager and procurement personnel, this strategy would enable the main focus in Ireland to be on the more complex hardware development.

The core hardware team, established to transfer Mouseman Classic and Sensa from a concept into high quality products, comprised of eight key personnel; the core team leader, a mechanical design engineer, a manu-facturing engineer and a quality engineer, all based at Logitech Ireland, a marketing manager from Logitech US in California, an electronic engineer from Logitech Switzerland in Lausanne, the industrial designer who had worked on the earlier cordless Mouseman project from Montgomery Pfeiffer, a consultancy in San Francisco and the colour consultant from the Domus Academy in Milan. Although mostly working on the project in their home countries, each member of this core team would be in regular contact with each other and would all have a weekly conference meeting throughout the project. This core hardware development team was, in turn, to be supported by a number of other personnel who could be utilized as a resource as and when they were required. Primarily drawn from Logitech Ireland, these included a programme manager to monitor individual schedules, purchasing, vendor quality, incoming inspection and production personnel together with functional managers, particularly from mechanical engineering and manufacturing. Other support team members outside Ireland included marketing strategists and in-house R&D consultant engi-neers in the US and CAD technicians in Switzerland. In addition there were six sub-contractors who, as the project progressed, provided input as necessary. These were the toolmakers and a CAD bureau in Taiwan, the moulders in Ireland, cubic printers in England and France and a rapid prototyping facility in Scotland.

Coordinating all these personnel was therefore one of the key responsibili-ties of the core team leader who had to be able to pull people in and, just as importantly, push them out of the team as a resource whenever necessary. However this system would only work effectively if the core team leader had a good understanding of who to pull in and when to do it, for, in this project, he had to ensure that such personnel were involved early enough to be completely up to speed with the project's progress whenever they were needed. Fundamentally he had to make sure that the right people with the right skills were in the right place at the right time.

Communication

To enable as efficient a development as possible to occur, particular attention was also paid at the planning stage to the organization of communication both within the team and to and from outside. Every Thursday evening there would be a full team meeting using a conference call. This would provide a regular forum at which ideas could be discussed, problems could be identified and all members of the team updated on progress of all aspects of the project. These meetings would also provide the opportunity for individual senior managers to be kept abreast of developments on a weekly basis. However, unlike previous projects where meetings could go on for hours while all present ploughed through a lengthy agenda, with the Sensä project these sessions would sometimes only last for a few minutes so that once all the necessary items had been covered, the team members could each return to their planned programme and not waste time listening to largely independent discussions which could take place more effectively on a one-to-one basis.

To support such individual communication, the entire team was inter-linked by an internal electronic mail system through which details could be discussed at length. Rather than use the Internet which was at the time both insecure and largely limited to text-based communication, Logitech used Lotus Notes within which sketches, spreadsheets and drawings could all be attached to memos sent both to individual mailboxes and to a central project database open to all. Together with regular telephone and fax communication wherever necessary, this system meant that the whole team could theoretically operate as effectively as they would do if they were all in the same location and would therefore help to maintain team cohesion.

In addition to this technology-based communication there would be just two full meetings in Ireland at which the entire team were present. These would be at the the start of the project when the overall schedule was being discussed and at the end when the pre-production testing of the developed product was being undertaken. Individual team members, particularly the core team leader and the mechanical designer, would also visit the USA and Taiwan for a number of weeks at critical stages such as the industrial design/ mechanical design and mechanical design/tooling interfaces, but, in the main, the need for the whole team to spend valuable time flying back and forth over the Atlantic would be kept down to the absolute minimum.

Whilst this would all help to ensure effective intra-team communication, additional information transfer would also be required outside the core team, primarily with other Logitech personnel. The planned channel for communication with senior management would occur through a series of product review committee meetings. However, should other issues which required approval, such as the need for extra funding or a major change in either the product or the packaging, arise between these meetings then the core team leader would act as the principal communication route. Communication with support members of the team, external consultants and sub-contractors would be undertaken by both the core team leader and individual team members as appropriate whenever necessary.

Product development

With this organizational system and structure in place, the development of the Mouseman could then proceed. The project was planned in detail and an overall schedule (Figure C3.2) prepared to indicate what tasks were to

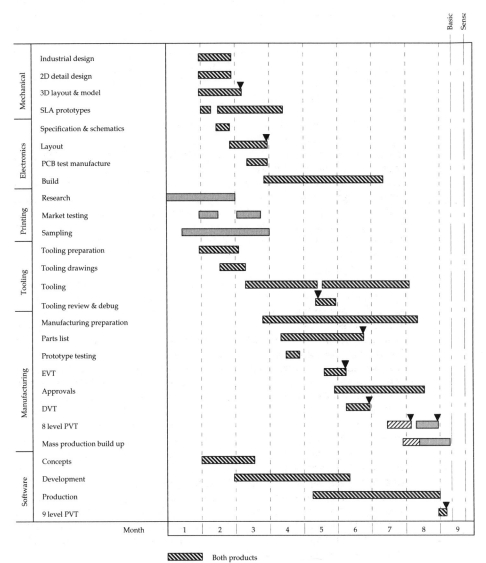

Figure C3.2 Logitech Mouseman Sensa project schedule

be undertaken, by whom and when. The project would involve six key areas of work:

- mechanical and industrial design of the upper mouldings, the base, the key-plate and interlock details;
- design and testing of the electronic circuitry;
- assessment of cubic printing and determination of four colour, pattern, texture combinations for the premium product;
- preparation of 3D CAD models and production drawings and the subsequent manufacture of tooling in Taiwan;
- preparation for manufacture including a series of verification tests leading to the ramp up to full scale production; and
- design, development and production of manuals and packaging.

Some of these would be able occur simultaneously whilst others would have to follow the traditional sequential approach.

Although they had previously adopted a cross-project phase review system with review meetings occurring at regular intervals, Logitech had found this difficult to implement when using a concurrent approach as it was hard to clearly identify where one phase ended and another began and so, by 1994 they had simplified it to a series of separate reviews by a project review committee. Comprising the business unit manager, senior managers to assess their individual functions' areas of work and a number of internal marketing and R&D consultants to provide a strategic input, this committee would look for a reassurance that the project was on schedule, within budget and would meet the planned specification. If they were satisfied that all three of these criteria had been met then approval would be given for continuation. During this project there were to be nine reviews; two in March to assess mechanical and electronic layout, a tooling review in May, two verification test reviews and a parts list review in June and final verification test reviews for the hardware and software in August and September. Product introduction was envisaged to occur in October 1994 but, as this was several months later than had been originally intended, the core team leader was therefore already under pressure to pull this date back. He was however reluctant to agree to an earlier PAD date at this time because of the unknowns involved, particularly regarding the cubic printing of the premium Sensa product, but undertook to examine them and come back to the product review committee with an updated schedule as soon as possible.

During January the consultant from the Domus Academy suggested twenty-five designs which he thought would be appropriate and recommended a process called cubic printing which enables plastics to be efficiently and cost-effectively coated with pattern, colour and texture to a very high standard. This process had been developed in Japan but was, at the time, licensed to only a few companies in Europe, of which one in France was recommended for initial samples. However, as cubic printing had been little used in the computer industry before, Logitech were unsure of how well it could be applied to their products and needed to investigate it further before committing themselves to this option.

The project started officially at the end of January. To ensure as smooth a transfer of data as possible, the mechanical design engineer first travelled to California to work with both marketing and the industrial designer on the preparation of preliminary industrial design specifications for the upper mouldings and while the industrial designer then worked with marketing throughout February, developing the external shape of the product in the USA, the mechanical designer returned to Ireland. There he started on the detailed design of the guts of the product, focusing particularly on the potentially problematic area of the key plate, the base of the product onto which all the main components are mounted. In anticipation, as an advanced project in January, he had already assessed the design of key plates in all Logitech's previous mice and the competition's products. This had enabled him to identify a number of details which, if incorporated into Mouseman 2 from the start, would help ensure that the developed design would be more reliable in both moulding and assembly.

In parallel with this, marketing staff in California undertook some initial market testing of the twenty-five different colour/texture/pattern proposals for the premium product which had by then been sampled on existing Mouseman Cordless mouldings in France. These samples were used in market clinics established in three large shopping malls to see what combinations appealed to potential consumers. This process very quickly enabled the original twenty-five designs to be reduced down to eight which were felt to be most popular. Ten samples of each of these were subsequently ordered for more detailed testing scheduled to take place in March.

At the end of the month, the core team leader and quality engineer visited the only two European companies which were considered to be capable of undertaking cubic printing in the required volumes. These were the French company which had already been used for the first samples and a competitor based in England. The concerns over the process and its applicability to computer mice had to be resolved quickly and so the capabilities of both the companies and the process itself were assessed in detail. After examining wear and colour degradation, the verdict on cubic printing was that it would withstand the expected high level of contact associated with mice and it was decided that it would be appropriate for the product. However, although impressed by the samples produced for the market testing, it was felt that the French company was less controllable than their English rivals who additionally claimed a higher capacity, were used to dealing with organizations like Logitech who demanded the highest quality and, because of their location, were also easier to support from Ireland. The English company was therefore selected exclusively at the end of the month and the necessary planning of schedules for printing of the production mouldings was initiated.

Simultaneously the manufacturing engineer and a senior mechanical engineering manager determined which toolmaker would be the most appropriate for this project. A Taiwanese firm was selected because they also had very good engineering capabilities, were competitive, could guarantee a high quality product, also had experience of working for western manufacturers such as Philips and, significantly, were prepared to work exclusively on the Mouseman tools for the duration of the project.

Concurrently with these hardware design activities, in the USA, marketing had also started working with the graphics consultant on concepts for the packaging and manuals for both the premium products and the mid-range version, both of which had recently been named. The printed models would be known as Mouseman Sensa while, to retain consistency, the basic model would retain the existing Mouseman name now widely associated with Logitech.

By March, the electronic engineer had begun designing the circuitry in Switzerland and the industrial design was complete. To assist both design verification and initial marketing testing, the mechanical engineer created a 3D CAD model to check the design and enable production of stereolithographic prototypes and vacuum cast models, by a rapid prototyping facility in Scotland. In partnership with the manufacturing engineer, the mechanical engineer also completed the production of initial part drawings which were transferred to a CAD bureau in Taiwan, which had been selected because of their high level of technical proficiency and close relationship with the toolmaker. Here fully detailed drawings and an updated 3D model in DUCT were all quickly produced to ensure that the data was efficiently transferred from 'design' to 'manufacture' without any delay for iterations.

Being controlled directly by the core team leader and programme manager in Ireland, this effort up front was deemed necessary as manufacturing needed to be able to go into high-volume production as soon as possible to meet the required volumes of stock by the PAD (product availability date; see page 92) which, because of the increased confidence in the cubic printing process, was now brought forward to September. Following the production of a schedule from the toolmaker based on receiving the data in March, it was agreed that PAD for the basic product would be in the first week of September with the premium product following on two weeks later.

While the tooling was taking place in Taiwan, initial layouts of the proposed production facility were being discussed in Ireland, electronic design was continuing in Switzerland and, in the US, marketing were carrying out a second set of customer user surveys of the eight different designs for the premium product. Samples were taken to five user clinics across the country where computer users were asked what they thought of a number of designs including the various cubic printed products, some painted grey to represent the planned basic model and a selection of competing products. The objective was to determine how highly people ranked colour, pattern and texture and the perceptions of the shape against the competition, and whether or not they would be prepared to pay more for a colour/texture/ pattern combination which they liked. The results of this testing showed that people would pay a small premium for this and the preference for the adopted shape was again confirmed. The eight sampled designs had now been reduced down to four, two with a soft feel texture and two with a high gloss. This subsequently helped to determine a Mouseman 2 product range comprising a mid-range basic version in a plain grey and four high-end Sensa cubic printed products.

By April the electronic design and test PCB manufacture was complete and build for the verification tests had been initiated while, in the USA, the packaging concepts were being developed. In Ireland purchasing deals were being made with the cubic printers and, having been in Taiwan for the transfer of data to the toolmaker, the mechanical design engineer returned to work with manufacturing and production staff to ensure that all the design details were understood and both the manual and automated assembly processes could be planned and the necessary equipment purchased. In addition moulders were being selected and prepared to take delivery of the tooling from Taiwan in early July. Of particular concern to the team was a desire to choose an Irish moulder, located close to a reliable toolmaker who could, if necessary, undertake any modification of the tooling that was required after sampling. Because moving the tooling about would take more time than moving people, it was felt to be more important to ensure that these two sub-contractors were both compatible and co-located than for either to necessarily be on Logitech's doorstep. In the end two companies in the Irish midlands, four hours' drive from Cork but only half an hour from each other were selected.

Having supported the toolmaker from Ireland for six weeks, in May the mechanical design and manufacturing engineers and the core team leader all travelled to Taiwan for the first samples to come off the tools. While the mechanical engineer subsequently identified and resolved a few minor problems with the design of the mouldings, the manufacturing engineer examined the tooling, looking at problems which might affect achieving a high yield from the tools together with tool construction details which might have been a problem to the Irish moulder. This planned parallel debug took about a month, far shorter than was, at the time, conventional for the industry and helped to maintain the shortened timescale.

As this was taking place in Taiwan, the core team leader returned to Ireland for the first of the product validation tests. Logitech have three such validation tests – engineering, design and process – all of which must be passed before full-scale production can be initiated. The first of these, the engineering validation test, used products based on the first samples to confirm that the basic form, fit and function of the product and its components were to specification and, subsequently, enabled these samples to be sent to all the relevant certification bodies for approval – a process which can take several months and therefore had to be started as early as possible. This was passed and, once a few necessary minor modifications had been made to the tooling, further samples were produced in Taiwan and sent to Ireland to be used for the design verification test which took place in the middle of June. This involved a small batch build of product on the production line undertaken by manufacturing, not to assess the assembly process but to check the design of the product for subtle problems related to high-volume mouldings. This was also passed with the need for only a few very minor changes which were quickly made as the project progressed on to the next stage.

Over the next few weeks the tooling was transported to Ireland and set up enabling the first samples made under local conditions to be produced and used for the process verification test, the final major hurdle before full-scale production. In the first week of August 1000 units were built in the now fully operative assembly facility, 500 on a manual line and 500 on an automated line. Evaluating the entire hardware production process, this test was trouble free and enabled full production of the basic product to start, with the premium Sensa product following on two weeks later as scheduled.

The design and production of the chosen packaging had by now also been completed in the USA, manuals had been written, translated and printed in Switzerland and the software was being duplicated in Ireland. Another process verification for the nine-level material therefore took place in the last week of August bringing together the assembled product, the box, manual and disc for the first time. Although a transparent clam shell which had been developed for the premium product turned out to be more awkward to put together than had been envisaged, this test was also passed and the necessary quantities of packaged product produced to enable the PAD dates for both models to be successfully achieved on target in September.

The Mouseman Sensa was launched worldwide in October 1994 and by the end of the year was selling over 140,000 units per month, making it the market leader within three months. By identifying colour, texture and pattern as added value features, Logitech were able to develop the mouse market, initiating a new direction in product differentiation and increasing their own product range.

Summary

This case study illustrates a number of key issues involved in the organization, planning and undertaking of a successful development project. It shows the benefits that can be gained by putting in place a fundamental structure designed to support the development of a new product by a core team chosen to provide the required foundation for the development process. It shows the need for a clear project focus and how, by ensuring that all tasks are appropriately scheduled, a realistic project timetable which can be successfully achieved can be compiled. It also demonstrates the importance of making sure that the team is appropriately resourced, not only by funding and equipment but also in terms of information and the use of additional personnel as and when they are required. In particular, it indicates the advantages of ensuring that the key people are able to work on the project full time without distractions either from other projects or by external influences and how, by having non-core project tasks re-allocated to support staff, they are themselves able to focus their attention on the project. It highlights the attention paid to the key data transition between the industrial designer and the mechanical engineer early on and, later, from the core team to the CAD bureau and toolmaker in

Taiwan to make sure that both occur as smoothly as possible. Finally and perhaps most importantly, it also provides a very good example of the role of an effective core team leader in managing the project and driving it forward, holding the team together and shielding it from unnecessary distractions and how, by selecting a project leader without a functional bias, he was able to ensure that all aspects of the project progressed on target with sufficient time to provide quality support, thus enabling the successful production and launch of a new product on time.

4 Rapid product development

Introduction

With the exception of a select few products such as the VW Beetle and the Zippo cigarette lighter which achieve cult status or long term mass appeal, over the past half century manufacturers have had to develop new products on a regular basis. Whereas the above products have been found to have the particular qualities which gave them a timeless appeal to a significant number of purchasers to allow them to continue in production, as the demands of the marketplace constantly change, the vast majority of products need to be continuously improved and updated to enable the necessary volumes of sales to justify their profitable manufacture to be achieved.

The advances in technology such as transistors and composite materials that have been made in the past fifty years have made many of the products which were produced previously largely redundant. Valve amplifiers and wooden tennis rackets are no longer mass market products and have been replaced by significantly improved developments. If we consider just one product sector, computers used in the home environment, and how it changed in one decade, we see a continuous development occurring taking us from the earliest Sinclair ZX80 running the simplest of BASIC programs to today's high performance PCs with Windows found in most students' bedrooms. In parallel with this, the improvements which have been made to the manufacturing processes themselves in terms of increased automation, greater productivity and production flexibility and in the correspondingly higher quality of products have all contributed to a reduction in real manufacturing costs and led to an increase in the number and variety of products which are now on the market.

This array of improvements to the manufacture of products has in turn made it easier to establish new and profitable manufacturing facilities all over the world. This has consequently enabled many previously non-industrialized countries to develop significant manufacturing bases which in many areas can and do compete with the best that Europe and the USA can offer. By implication this has therefore led to more and more competition, not only in the international export markets but also in previously more stable domestic markets. As a result, in order to survive let alone continue to grow, many western manufacturers have had to both continuously update their old products and also develop new ones. Only by doing this can their market shares be maintained, turnover increased and, assuming increasing productivity, higher profits generated.

This chapter gives an introduction to some of the key issues associated with the rapid development of new products. Following an initial introduction addressing the need for companies to develop new products on a regular basis, it details the reasoning behind companies' wish to develop products in shorter and shorter periods and explains some of the financial, market and resources advantages that stand to be gained from successful rapid product development. It then goes on to question how this can be achieved and identifies the need for a balance of attention to the organization and management of the process, the use of applicable enabling technologies and the importance of utilizing skilled and experienced development teams. Particular mention is made of the new computer-based technologies including solid modelling and the varied rapid prototyping and rapid tooling techniques.

New product development performance

If we consider the typical post-launch product life-cycle (Figure 4.1) the problem faced by most manufacturing companies lies not only with accelerating the period of initial sales growth after launch and maintaining the period of sales maturity for as long as possible but also in reducing the

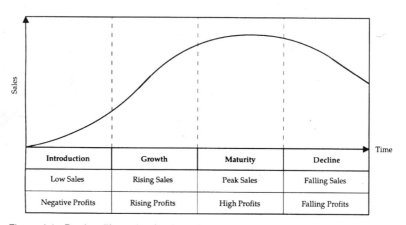

Figure 4.1 Product life-cycle after launch

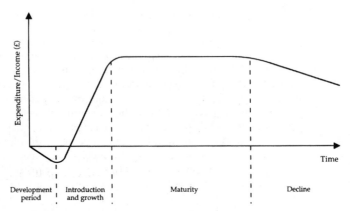

Figure 4.2 Ideal product life-cycle

costly development time which occurs before launch. In an idealized product life-cycle (Figure 4.2) the product development period is short and therefore product development costs are low. The introduction/growth period is also short and steep with sales reaching their peak quite soon, thereby maximizing revenue. The maturity period lasts for some time, giving the company an extended period of profits and the period of decline is slow meaning that when sales do eventually subside, profits fall gradually. However unfortunately, many companies face far less attractive scenarios. In the worst case (Figure 4.3), the development time is long and the development costs are high; the introduction/growth period is long and shallow; the maturity period is short and the decline is fast. In this situation the return on the investment is marginal with income barely exceeding

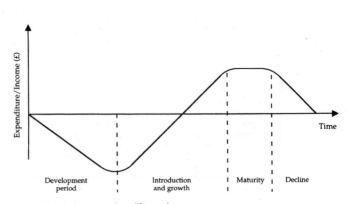

Figure 4.3 Worst-case product life-cycle

expenditure. This type of occurrence is particularly common in those companies manufacturing high-technology products dependent on significant R&D effort such as computer hardware and where the market is heavily influenced by rapid technological change.

In order to help them address some of the key issues involved in new product development and identify how to move closer to the idealized scenario, some companies have developed the relatively simple product life-cycle concept into a sophisticated analytical tool. One such organization is Hewlett Packard who back in 1987 developed what became known as the return map (Figure 4.4). This composite representation depicts not only investment in product development and the returns from that investment, but also the elapsed time to develop the product, introduce it and achieve the desired returns. Used as an ongoing monitor of a product development programme and involving all functions, it tracks costs and revenues and provides key measures such as break-even time, time to market, break-even after release and, most importantly, the return factor by which a project's progress can be evaluated. It therefore gives a detailed summary of new product development performance and is used as a basis for many of the strategic decisions within the company. This became the staple of Hewlett Packard's product development cycle and

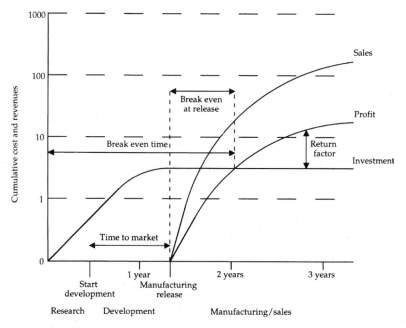

Figure 4.4 Hewlett Packard return map

has now also been adopted by a number of other companies including Philips where it now forms a core part of their ongoing restructuring and revitalization programme.

Rapid product development

However, even with this level of analysis, a major aim of most companies remains the development of products which follow the ideal life-cycle shown in Figure 4.2 rather than that in Figure 4.3. Having a 'world class' product which clearly addresses the identified needs of the marketplace is one means of theoretically ensuring that, after launch, growth of sales is rapid and the highly profitable maturity period is extended for as long as possible. However, particularly in the last few years, the increasingly global competitive market in not only the familiar consumer products, electronics and automotive sectors, but also in capital goods, machine tools and medical equipment, has focused attention on getting the product to launch quickly – reducing the time to market and, as the key means of achieving this – much effort has been and is being made to reduce the length of the development period.

If a company can successfully reduce the development period, the advantages that stand to be gained are threefold:

- First (Figure 4.5), it can be seen that being early to market and specifically earlier to market than the competition, enables an earlier return on the investment to be achieved. Although it is not always cheaper to develop

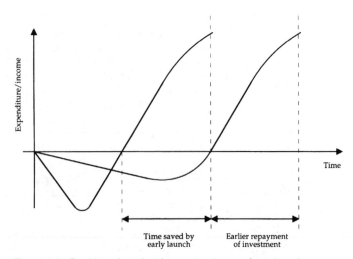

Figure 4.5 Rapid product development: return on investment

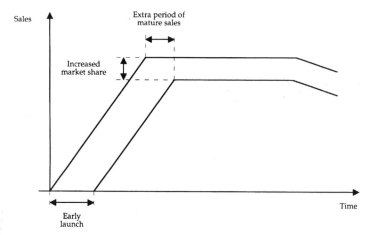

Figure 4.6 Rapid product development: sales and market share

a product in six months rather than a year, by being on the market six months early, products can be sold, income received and, in some cases, the entire development costs repaid by the end of the year. By any financial measure, there is no doubt that this alone can be judged to be a benefit worth pursuing.

- Second, this earlier launch also provides the opportunity for greater financial return over the whole product life (Figure 4.6). By being the first to launch a new product, manufacturers usually manage to achieve a larger market share, not only in the first few months but often throughout production. Although always vulnerable to higher-performance, lower-cost new products which may be developed by the competition, by putting high-quality products on the shelves first, some companies also find that high market share can be maintained. Furthermore, even if, after some time overall sales in the product sector may subside, this early advantage can still be carried through, the higher market share is maintained and the return on the initial investment maximized. More-over, in some cases the early launch also leads to a longer mature sales period than would have been otherwise expected, which further extends the overall period during which the higher financial return continues to exist.

- Lastly by simply speeding up product development, manufacturers also free their resources for other projects (Figure 4.7). For example, reducing the development period for a new car from say three years to eighteen months not only enables Ford, GM or Rover to launch a new model eighteen months early and potentially achieve the benefits described above, but it also means that in the second eighteen months another new car can be designed, developed and launched. Clearly by spending less

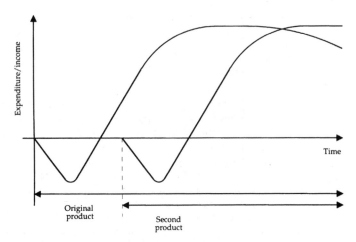

Figure 4.7 Rapid product development: multiple projects

time on one development project, any company can therefore increase the number of new products being developed. This serves to increase the number of products on the market, increase the income from sales and therefore increase the overall turnover and profits generated by the company.

However in some instances, this is unfortunately not a long-term luxury, for as the competition also develop their products more and more quickly, the importance of developing not only wholly new products but also continuously improving the most recent versions becomes more and more critical. Taking Ford as an example, it can be seen that although the Sierra was on the market for over ten years, to maintain its market share, throughout that time it was updated a number of times and, as the period required to redesign the car became shorter and shorter, these updates occurred more and more frequently. This principle applies equally to products such as ICL computers, Panasonic videos and Whiskas cat food and it is clear that it is only by increasing the speed of the product development process, that companies can develop more and more new products, maintaining their competitive edge and thereby obtain the advantages that have been highlighted.

Achieving rapid product development

The question therefore is how is rapid product development actually being achieved? What methods and procedures are being adopted and what devices are available to help companies reduce their development periods?

Basically many manufacturers across industry are now beginning to adopt the same generic principles in three key areas: organization, technology and skills.

Organization

As discussed previously, over the past few years the most significant change that has occurred from an organizational perspective has been the clear move towards concurrent engineering and the use of multi-disciplinary teams operating in a simultaneous timeframe, ideally working in partnership with subcontractors and involving suppliers in the development of the product. As shown in Figures 3.6 and 3.8, by enabling operations such as design development and testing to be undertaken in parallel wherever possible, the various stages of the process can overlap and therefore by implication the overall development period can be reduced. Although some tasks still cannot begin until decisions have been made in earlier phases of the development, the potential exists to dramatically decrease the overall time spent on product development. However it should be recognized that this has really only been applied to the core development activities and not the more 'fuzzy front end' pre-development stages. Because rapid product development relies on accurate projections of individual tasks' time scales, it is very difficult to accommodate stages such as idea generation which can take anything from a few days to several years depending on the product, the market and the organization. Therefore it is also more common for rapid product development to be practised for incremental innovation projects where an existing product exists, improvements can be identified and the necessary changes accurately evaluated and scheduled.

As well as this relatively recent change in the organization of new product development, there are two other elements within the process which can be considered to contribute significantly to enabling rapid product development to occur. These are the technology that can be used to improve it and the skills required by the individuals who are utilized to undertake it.

Technology

In addition to adopting organizational and methodological procedures to reduce the time to market for a new product, there are a large number of technologies which have been developed to aid rapid product development which can be of benefit to manufacturers. Some enable the overall quality of the design and hence the end product to be increased and others serve to decrease the cost of progressing the product into manufacture. However for most companies, technology is only of interest if it truly makes product development both better and faster and also reduces costs in every respect. It is of no use if it merely replaces existing practice with no significant improvements. It is therefore the correct use of appropriate enabling technology which allows the product development process to be improved and can in turn help to make manufacturing companies more competitive.

CAD

The first companies to take advantage of CAD did so in the mid-1980s, the main use at that time being for 2D draughting where the ability to change elements of the designs allowed repeatedly high quality drawings to be economically and efficiently produced and modified. Although at this stage many manufacturers considered it inappropriate to buy their own systems, both doubting that they would provide any great advantage over the traditional drawing board approach and considering that the time taken to learn the packages would make their overall use uneconomic. But, nevertheless, a small number of companies did gradually make the jump and acquired CAD systems such as PAFEC's DOGS whilst others also installed early versions of IBM's Catia 3D modelling system and CAEDS finite element analysis by SDRC.

Since then, the use of CAD within design has grown steadily. The gradual reduction in relative purchase costs, the continued increase in performance of the machines, the rise in the number of facilities available to designers, the development of the user orientated interfaces associated with Microsoft's Windows and Apple Computers and improved communication between the varied software, have all led to an expansion in the uptake of CAD systems throughout industry.

Today a high proportion of companies now operate some sort of CAD system such as Autocad, ME10 or Euclid running on a variety of different platforms ranging from PCs and Macs to Silicon Graphics and Hewlett Packard workstations. Although still largely used by many for 2D applications, there are some which have been extended into basic 3D modelling and analysis coupled with NC and CNC machines to allow a level of CADCAM capability. However it should be acknowledged that despite the advantages of 2D CAD systems in terms of the quality of drawings, etc., they do sometimes force designers to think in two dimensions, thereby potentially restricting their creativity. Therefore much importance has recently been placed on the development of systems which offer true three dimensional modelling capabilities.

3D modelling

Perhaps the single most important advance which has been made in technology to aid rapid product development is the use of 3D solid modelling packages. Today, the effective use of capable modelling software is a key ingredient to successfully achieving the level of product development proficiency necessary to compete in the future. The range of facilities available has grown considerably since the earliest wire-frame based systems of the early 1980s to a point where a number of competing products now offer the development team the capacity to not only produce 3D computer models at the detail design stage but also aid earlier conceptual work and, more commonly, considerably improve the transfer of product data from the designers to toolmakers, sub-contractors, suppliers and manufacturing and assembly facilities.

Systems such as Parametric's Pro Engineer and SDRC's IDEAS allow the speed of product development potentially to be increased significantly. First by giving the designers a sophisticated design capability throughout the project, they can deliver models of a far greater accuracy than traditionally available. Additionally they allow the designers to examine individual components in detail way in advance of production, identify problems and therefore improve the potential for them to be manufactured 'right first time'.

For designers, the latest solid modelling software also gives them the previously unavailable ability to deal with complex surfaces, thereby potentially allowing them the opportunity to become more creative in their designs. Moreover the fact that these systems rely on one coherent database for the 3D models, the 2D projections and drawings as well as the varied analytical facilities and the data that can be downloaded to rapid prototyping and tooling systems, means that, compared to wire-frame and surface modelling packages, there is an significant improvement in both the control of the design and the ease of its modification at any stage.

Rapid prototyping and tooling

Following on from this increasing use of 3D solid modelling within the development process there has been much recent advocation of the advantages to be gained from the use of a variety of different processes referred to collectively as rapid prototyping and tooling. By using appropriate technologies to model accurately prototype components in a fraction of the time taken by usual methods, designs can be assessed in detail well before tooling is completed and manufacture is begun. Whereas it may for example take several weeks of traditional manual machining to create a component for evaluation and testing, by using rapid prototyping techniques highly accurate 3D models can be built in a matter of hours. Utilizing the data available from the 3D modelling packages discussed previously enables physical models, identical to the original CAD data, to be produced very quickly. These models not only allow design and manufacturing to evaluate the developed design in terms of ease of manufacture and its fulfilment of the desired objectives, but also enable marketing potentially to have a range of models for testing early on and for customers to actually see and hold the developed product way in advance of full-scale production. In addition, the availability of accurate 3D models of proposed designs to support drawings and computer models also helps to reduce some of the misunderstandings between the various functions that are involved in product development teams.

Furthermore, having these models available at such a relatively early stage also permits any necessary revisions to the design to be easily accommodated. Whereas with conventional prototyping techniques, the costs and time scales involved usually meant that any changes caused significant delay and expense to the project, adopting rapid prototyping techniques enables even major revisions to be made to the CAD data and new models produced within only a few days. It can also be argued that the use of such technology also gives development teams more creative freedom. As they are able not only quickly to evaluate designs in 3D but also easily create a range of models of alternative designs, more opportunity is therefore available for the identification of problems and for more innovative solutions to be subsequently generated. Together, all these benefits have encouraged a number of companies such as Apple to now use rapid prototyping techniques on virtually all their products. In addition, having the ability to provide toolmakers with accurate models of the proposed components for quotation purposes frequently encourages discussion of improvements to specific details which may be possible to make manufacture more efficient and often results in cheaper quotes than would be given on the basis of drawings and CAD data alone.

However, as well as being used to make models of components, the same technology can also provide manufacturers with the means of producing initial tooling in extremely short time scales. By creating the tooling directly or using the initial model to produce a resin mould, numerous sample components in a range of different materials which in turn mimic others can easily and quickly be manufactured. This has the dual advantage of both creating prototype components which replicate the performance and characteristics of the intended product and also maximizing the benefits gained from the use of the technology to create the original.

As indicated above, the various rapid prototyping and tooling technologies are all essentially dependent on the integration of computers within the development process and, by utilizing the available data, create models in two different ways: NC and CNC milling cut-away from an initial block of material to leave a 3D representation of a component whilst a number of other, more recent, technologies achieve the same result by building the model up one layer at a time. Vendors of any of these processes commonly identify a host of features which make their particular method of producing a prototype appear to be the best. However, as with many other areas of technology application, it is a case of horses for courses and the decision of which to use is dependent on the intended application.

As summarized in Table 4.1 below, if you are for example seeking to produce a number of large components then solid ground curing could be considered to be the most appropriate technology; however, if you are after

Table 4.1

	Process	Applications
SLA	Stereolithography	Accurate complex components
SGC	Solid ground curing	Large components in volume
LOM	Laminated object manufacturing	Accurate patterns for casting
FDM	Fused deposition modelling	Low cost bench-top models
SLS	Selective laser sintering	Investment casting
DSC	Direct shell casting	Metal moulds and castings

very accurate complex components then stereolithography is a widely preferred option. On the other hand if you are looking to make patterns for casting, laminated object manufacturing could be the one, or, better still, once it becomes fully available commercially, direct shell casting.

Fundamentally the choice needs to be made in consultation with the service providers but whichever of this increasing variety of processes is selected, the overall principle of producing prototype components quickly remains the same.

These techniques can all be used to accelerate the design to production transfer stage of a project, and by enabling problems such as interference between mouldings to be easily identified and amended before the tooling is cut, the expensive and time consuming iterations that frequently occur at this late stage of a project can be eliminated. They therefore play an important role in enabling rapid product development to occur, but they do not, as some are unfortunately led to believe, offer a complete solution in themselves. Instead they have to be used in partnership with other compatible technology, effective organization and planning of the development process and equally as significant, the particular skills and experience of the development teams.

Skills

Although it may initially appear that the range of new technology available from 3D modelling to rapid prototyping techniques mean that, when combined with the necessary organizational and managerial structures, it becomes relatively simple to develop new products quickly, in reality this is not the case. There is one more critical component in the rapid product development portfolio without which any project will never achieve its full potential. This is the skills and experience of the development team, the individuals whose particular talents enable the technology to be used to maximum benefit and who are in essence the linchpin of any project.

Despite all the technology now available, product development is at its heart still a creative process and whether undertaken in house or externally, it is important for manufacturers to be aware of the value of the designer's creativity. In the earliest stages of a development programme, no available technology can yet replace the initial creativity of the designers in the production of innovative and diverse product concepts. No matter what some may claim, nothing can beat pencil and paper as the optimum means of communicating and visualizing ideas and until there is software which enables computer models to be truly as flexible as clay, it is doubtful whether any professional designer will even begin to put away these basic tools. Concept sketches provide the creative foundation upon which the later use of the technology to achieve rapid product development can be built. Without this input from skilled designers, the chances of developing anything other than mediocre products is significantly reduced.

Many manufacturers have the internal resources available to establish and maintain development teams equipped with the necessary facilities to enable effective rapid product development to occur successfully. Existing design staff who have the creative skills and are already familiar with CAD technology can be trained to use new modelling software and prototyping techniques and, when incorporated into well-organized multi-disciplinary teams, can perform their development roles effectively. Some of these companies, like Rover Group, have gone so far as to purchase their own stereolithography equipment linked to suites of workstations, whilst others have chosen to use one of the specialist rapid prototyping bureaux that are now operating throughout the world. For these companies their main areas of focus are now on topics such as further improving the management and organization of their development teams and on areas such as more effective market research and better development of specifications at the front end of the process.

However, many other companies who can also benefit from achieving more rapid product development are often in a situation where they are unable to purchase the facilities and have neither the time or the money available to train their existing designers to become competent in their use. For other manufacturers, product development may be cyclical and therefore the need for full-time design teams cannot be justified. For all these, the option of buying in the necessary expertise is becoming more and more attractive and a number of specialists are becoming available to provide these services. Not only do they have the required skills to be fully effective from 'day 1', but, as most have their own equipment, there is no additional resource demand placed upon the manufacturer. Several organizations now offer companies a contract option where they can arrive, set up their equipment, perform the desired tasks and leave having completed the work, all within very short time scales. Additionally, to enable them to make more use of their equipment and expertise, several other organizations including a number of universities are also offering design bureau services to industry. In some circumstances such options as these can be an effective and cost efficient means of accessing the technology required to achieve more rapid product development, but as sub-contractors these organizations are rarely integrated within development teams and, in some cases, do not offer the same level of skills that would be available from a third option of using full-time commercial design consultancies.

There are now a wide selection of established design groups who have the facilities and expertise to help manufacturers achieve the successful rapid product development. In addition to the technology, they also offer their clients the added advantage of years of successful creative design practice. Many have been involved with the development of a wide range of successful products for a variety of international manufacturers and over the years have developed their knowledge and understanding of the key elements involved in successful product design. Moreover, as they are constantly working in the field of new product development, they are used to operating in the environment and culture associated with rapid product development and can, at times, also be a useful source of new ideas and interpretations.

Whichever of these alternatives is considered to be the most appropriate, it is clearly vital that this third piece of the jigsaw is not neglected. A company can change its structure, adopt new management techniques and buy new equipment, but without a skilled and experienced internal or external design resource, the chances of successfully developing products within ever shorter time scales are remote.

Chapter summary

This chapter has given an overview of some of the key factors associated with rapid product development. The advantages that can be achieved on a company's new product development performance have been outlined. The organizational requirements have been reiterated and the varied technologies available to enable rapid product development to occur have been identified. In addition the need to ensure that this technology is professionally utilized has been underlined. From these it is clear that the key to successfully achieving the rapid development of products which will succeed in the marketplace and take full advantage of the benefits outlined here lies in the correct combination of the issues that have been addressed:

- By being early to market with a well designed product companies can obtain a greater return on their investment.
- Rapid product development gives a potential to achieve an increased market share and an extended sales life, as well as freeing resources for more projects.
- To achieve this the appropriate organizational structure and cultures have to be adopted to enable true concurrent engineering to take place.
- The applicable enabling technologies such as solid modelling, stereolithography and vacuum casting need to be accessed and used.
- Development teams need to have the necessary skills and experience to use the relevant technologies both creatively and efficiently.
- Only by recognizing all of these areas can manufacturers significantly improve the design and performance of their products, enabling them to compete successfully in both domestic and international markets and reap the rewards that are available.

References

Crawford, C.M. (1992) The Hidden Costs of Accelerated Product Development. *Journal of Product Innovation Management*, **9**, 188–199.

House, C.A. and Price, R.L. (1991) The Return Map: Tracking Product Teams. *Harvard Business Review*, **69**, 1, 92–100.

McDonough, E.F.M. (1993) Faster New Product Development: Investigating the Effects of Technology and Characteristics of the Project Leader and Team. *Journal of Product Innovation Management*, **10**, 241–250.

Smith, P.G. and Reinertsen, D.G. (1991) *Developing Products in Half the Time*. Van Nostrand Reinhold.

Case study 4: Polaroid Spectra instant camera

Polaroid is a multinational corporation based in Boston. Since 1937 when the company was established, it has grown into one of the largest manufacturers of photographic equipment and now has production facilities operating in four countries generating an annual turnover of over $2000m.

The company's main product lines are primarily film and instant cameras for which they hold a number of worldwide patents. In the mid-1980s Kodak attempted to take a share of their market by launching their own version of the instant camera and were subsequently successfully sued for infringement of patents.

The existing range of instant cameras had been on the market for over ten years when in early 1993 sales began to decline and the need to revitalize the product was first identified. As the end of their original patent protection was also on the horizon, the company were anticipating rival products to appear, particularly from Japanese manufacturers such as Fujitsu, and was therefore keen to reinforce its position as market leader. In addition, there was also a stated requirement to develop a more exciting product for the company, whose image had recently become perceived as conventional and conservative.

Although the need to develop a new camera was identified at the beginning of 1993, it was not until the end of the year that the decision to go ahead was finally taken. By this time sales had begun to fall steeply and therefore, in order to maintain turnover and profits, the company had to develop and launch the new design as quickly as possible (Figure C4.1).

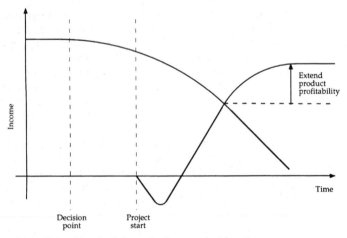

Figure C4.1 Polaroid – declining sales/new project impetus

Significantly, the company chose not to develop this product in the USA but instead the project was managed by their UK manufacturing facility located in the Vale of Leven in Scotland. This was the first time that a Polaroid product had been wholly developed by Polaroid UK.

This case history describes the rapid development of this new camera using the latest computer-based technology and manufacturing techniques in parallel with the principles of simultaneous engineering and teamwork.

The project

Although using the same optics that were present in their existing design and only upgrading a few elements of the electronics, as a means of differentiating the new product from the range developed in the 1980s, Polaroid sought to change significantly the visual and ergonomic details of the camera. They therefore asked the British Design Council to recommend design groups who would be able to assist. Of particular interest to the company when they were selecting the designers was their desire to undertake the project in as short a development period as possible and therefore they were looking for a consultancy able not only to provide the necessary creative input but one which also had the technical competence and ability to deliver a complete solution on an extremely tight schedule and also work as part of an international multi-disciplinary team.

Following recent work including the rapid development of a new telephone for Matsushita of Japan, Polaroid eventually chose London-based multi-disciplinary design group PDD. In addition to a strong track record in designing similar scale products for a range of manufacturers, Polaroid were specifically interested in the consultancy's use of some of the latest 3D modelling systems linked to rapid prototyping facilities to enable them to undertake projects such as this one in extremely compressed timescales.

Due to the importance of the project to Polaroid and their desire to undertake the development in as short a time period as possible, a multi-disciplinary development team was put together which utilized the varied areas of expertise available (Figure C4.2). The project was coordinated from the USA by a project manager who could draw on inputs from marketing, optics and electronics, manufacturing engineers and senior production and purchasing managers from the UK manufacturing facility in Strathclyde who provided the production engineering input and supplier knowledge. PDD in London, provided the design skills and rapid product development experience and a number of UK-based toolmakers and moulders gave manufacturing advice. All these were under the ultimate control of a programme controller in the US. This relatively flat structure enabled clear direct communication between disciplines and was particularly beneficial during periods of parallel working when, in anticipation of the end result, early decisions were being made on partial data. One aspect of the organization of this project which was found to be especially useful was the fact that although the project manager was US based, he also took an active role in the team, promoting communication.

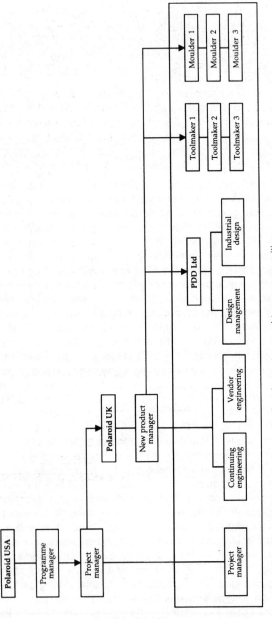

Figure C4.2 Polaroid project – organizational structure and team composition

Briefing

An initial design brief was issued by Polaroid in December 1993 and, in consultation with PDD, this was developed into a complete document, detailing phases of work, cost information timescales and a project schedule (Figure C4.3). This illustrates the aim to complete the entire project within nine months, enabling launch of the product worldwide with sufficient stock in the shops in October 1994.

The development began officially in January 1994 with a two-day briefing in Scotland where, in addition to clarification of the design brief and product specification, the designers from PDD were able to gain a thorough understanding of the production techniques used to build the cameras. At this stage the design team were able to take away existing cameras, details of improvements that were being made to the optics and electronics and of

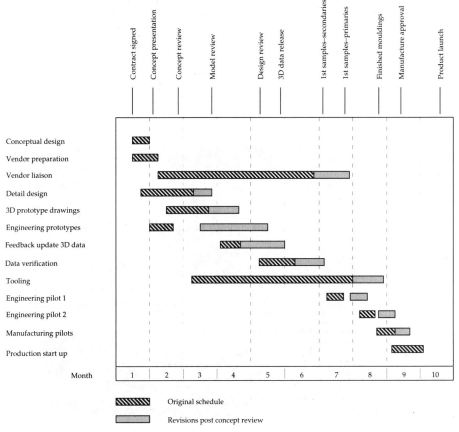

Figure C4.3 Polaroid – project schedule

particular use, a database of the original camera components created as a wireframe model in the early 1980s. As the success of the project depended in part on being able to produce the necessary data for tooling as early as possible, this information proved invaluable since the new mouldings were required to interface with the existing chassis so fit and interface details could easily be adopted.

Concept design

Although PDD make extensive use of computers in the development of new products, they believe that they do not encourage creativity in the early stages of design. Therefore all initial work on the Polaroid camera was carried out by hand using sketches (Figure C4.4) and model media in order to explore the complex surfaces and ergonomic relationships. They did use 2D design packages to support their concept design by checking that the necessary components fitted into the available spaces in the required configuration, but these did not directly influence the designs. However as a means of exploring the range of possible colour and graphic combinations, computer-based rendering packages were used to generate high-quality visuals.

Because the project was being undertaken on such a tight schedule, while designers were sketching concept designs, toolmakers who could produce the necessary tools direct from 3D data in less than ten weeks were being identified, data exchange established and orders placed. This was the only

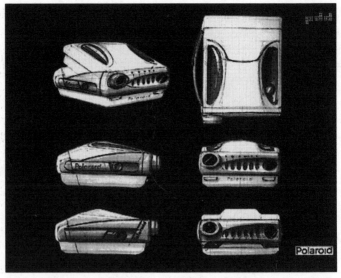

Figure C4.4 Concept sketches. Reproduced by kind permission of Pankhurst Design & Developments Limited

way that everything could be made ready in time for the project to be completed within nine months. To create the initial computer models for the development of the camera, the original wireframe model was first remodelled in a modern solid modelling system called IDEAS which would allow the designers greater control of fine details in the later stages of the project.

The concept work was presented to Polaroid in early February as a hand-built model and computer images, and the decision was taken to move directly into concept development. However following consultation with New York-based designers Henry Dreyfuss Associates who had undertaken some earlier concept work, a hybrid design resulted. Although this combined the best features of all the different concepts, it unfortunately led to the re-appraisal of almost every external face of the camera and the adoption of an entirely new handle, viewfinder and control area. This all introduced an unplanned delay to the project which, in order to meet the launch date would have to be clawed back during the rest of the programme.

Detail design

Following acceptance of the revised concept, engineering layouts of the new camera were prepared and initial 3D computer models (Figures C4.5 and C4.6) were released to toolmakers who were able to start tool design and prepare the metal bolsters from which, once they had been designed, the mouldings would be made. Throughout this period, as complex surfaced

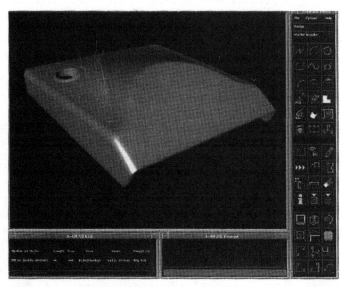

Figure C4.5 Component 3D model. Reproduced by kind permission of Pankhurst Design & Developments Limited

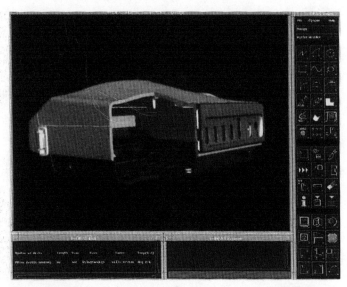

Figure C4.6   'Walkthrough'. Reproduced by kind permission of Pankhurst Design & Developments Limited

components were modelled on the computer to assess form and ergo-nomics, block models were produced using CNC machines working directly from the designers' software. By 5 April, the first components modelled and prototyped using a process called stereolithography were available, and during the month, a first working prototype was produced (Figure C4.7). This was used to assess not only the visual and ergonomic features but also the engineering design of the components and their fit to the existing camera chassis. Using this prototype and feedback from Polaroid's marketing department, a number of slight changes were identified and the required changes subsequently made to the the 3D computer models.

In May, Polaroid held a major design review which included all members of the design team, the programme manager, marketing representatives and production staff from the manufacturing plant. This review marked one of most important points in the project, for if it did not pass the design then the project would be delayed or worse, halted completely. The decisions taken here would be far reaching as they would dictate not only the future actions of the project team but also the operation of the entire manufacturing plant over the next few months, for it was necessary to create a final inventory of existing parts and product prior to tools being modified and production techniques changed for the manufacture of the new camera. The final design was presented for approval in prototype form using a model made using components produced by both CNC milling and stereolithography and screen shots from the 3D database (Figure C4.8), backed up with the now available prototype moulded components and engineering rigs. After a

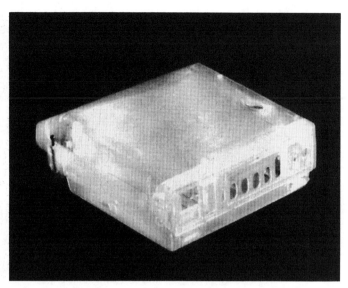

Figure C4.7 Stereolithographic model. Reproduced by kind permission of Pankhurst Design & Developments Limited

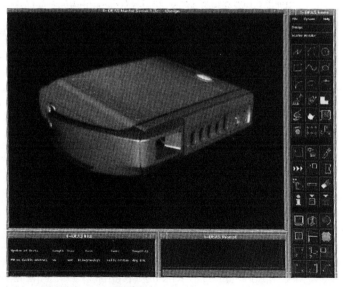

Figure C4.8 Full 3D model. Reproduced by kind permission of Pankhurst Design & Developments Limited

Figure C4.9 Prototype. Reproduced by kind permission of Pankhurst Design & Developments Limited

successful review, the design was passed with the addition of a few last minute minor changes that inevitably occur even at this stage of a project.

PDD were then commissioned to produce twelve working prototype cameras (Figure C4.9) which were made using vacuum castings produced from the original stereolithographic models. These cameras were required by Polaroid in order to carry dealer and distributor liaison and internal briefings as well as for photographic shoots to allow the production of promotion and packaging material. To stand a chance of regaining the now delayed schedule, it was decided immediately to release data to the toolmakers for production. As all the final prototype components had not yet been received and the database remained dimensionally unchecked this presented considerable risk, so it was agreed that the final release of data would be scheduled on a rolling basis over the following three weeks with any areas of change identified at the earliest opportunity.

Tooling

By the first week of June all the main database components had been released in their final form to the toolmakers and secondary components were to follow shortly. Having already carried out the tool design, determining tool actions and split lines from pre-release data the toolmakers were then able to concentrate on the creation of the individual tool cavities and inserts. At the same time, having had little opportunity for detailed component checking, PDD turned their efforts toward the production of 2D drawings of the new parts which, although not required for the purposes of production, were to be used to provide 'metal safe' information to the toolmakers.

With these areas defined, it was then possible to undertake a detailed dimensional assessment of the production database. This lasted through mid-June. The opportunity was then taken to make one final visual check of the form of the cutting electrode against early CNC database models to verify the quality of surface data prior to committing it to steel.

During the first week of July the less complex components were sampled for the first time from the new tools. These trials yielded the first moulded components to the new design and placed the demand upon PDD to prepare a further set of 2D drawings, this time exhibiting critical dimensions for the purposes of quality assurance and inspection. In mid-July sampling of the main mouldings began in earnest. These were generally produced by the toolmakers in order to avoid the need to ship large tools around the country to implement modifications.

Engineering pilot

After an initial on-site appraisal these mouldings were sent to Polaroid's manufacturing plant to be used in the first engineering pilot where, to identify any unforeseen problems, engineering staff built cameras using untextured metal safe mouldings. More importantly this also enabled the various tool

Figure C4.10 Final design. Reproduced by kind permission of Pankhurst Design & Developments Limited

tuning modifications to be defined. Although one of the least controlled operations of the whole project, the designers' experience combined with the use of simple engineering rigs enabled modifications to be defined with a minimum of iterations. After a series of cameras had been built, the tools were passed back to the tool room to implement the modifications, resample and, if necessary, modify further. Following this, all the tools were passed to a tool finishing company to have the specified textures photo-etched; this event was dictated by the desire to etch all tools simultaneously using the same vendor and thus eliminating any possibility of visual differences between mouldings marring the quality of the final product. This was controlled by the prime toolmaker who, at the initiation of the tooling cycle, had briefed all toolmakers to use identical tool steel from a common vendor. This was done to further ensure consistency of finish across the final product.

By the beginning of August, the finished tools were sampled for the final time and parts shipped to Polaroid for the second engineering pilot to check earlier modifications. This was followed by the manufacturing pilot where the first attempt was made at a production run of cameras (Figure C4.10). These were built, not by engineers, but by the manufacturing facility itself. This enabled production jigs and fixtures to be assessed and production staff to become familiar with the details of the new design.

Production

In mid-September the final hurdle for the new product was faced – the Polaroid approval for mass production. However this was somewhat short-circuited by initiating production start-up the week before in order to ensure that the

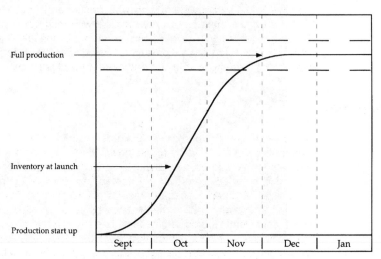

Figure C4.11 Polaroid production ramp up

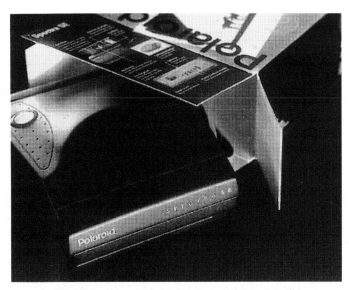

Figure C4.12 Production camera with packaging. Reproduced by kind permission of Pankhurst Design & Developments Limited

required inventory quantity as originally planned was successfully achieved. Whilst this review did not produce any major upsets, the few necessary improvements that were identified were incorporated within a second set of tools which were following on two weeks later. Production then ramped up through September guaranteeing that the required volume of cameras were available for the worldwide launch which occurred in mid-October (Figure C4.11): Polaroid therefore went to market with their latest product (Figure C4.12) – one designed, tooled and produced in the UK – in the shortest timescale that the company has ever achieved: six months from a blank sheet of paper to first samples and just nine months to full production inventory.

Summary

This contemporary case history illustrates a number of key features of rapid product development as it exists today. Primarily it shows that, if a well integrated team successfully adopt the principles of concurrent engineering supported by effective use of the appropriate technology, then successful product development can take place in relatively short timescales. It also clearly demonstrates not only the importance of detailed planning of the whole development programme from briefing to product launch, but also highlights the need for all parties involved to be adaptive so that the original project goals can be achieved, even when faced with a continually changing critical path.

Conclusion

Although only able to briefly introduce a few of the main issues associated with new product development today, this book has hopefully given an insight into some core aspects of the process. Within the context of a three-phase overall process outlined in the Introduction, the four main chapters have in turn discussed: how a new product development strategy is derived from overall corporate objectives and the chosen means of achieving them, the key role that innovation plays in the development of successful new products, the various organizational improvements that have been introduced to the process and, finally, why increasing the speed of development has become so important and how this is presently being achieved. But, while these chapters have provided an introduction to the respective subjects, further, more detailed information can be found in the growing number of publications dealing with each area individually, some of which have been cited in the references.

More importantly for this book and its reader are, however, the four main case studies associated with each chapter. These have each given a reliable representation of how the theory is currently being put into practice and, as, in the end, this is the intended focus, perhaps provide the most significant areas of information. Although new theories and new technologies to assist in the improvement of the effectiveness of new product development are continually being generated, the best way of judging which are the most appropriate is to look towards leading manufacturers and see which they are adopting. As leaders in their fields, Rover, Flymo, Logitech and Polaroid all provide very good indications of what approaches to product development are currently the most applicable in the real world.

As for any indication of the future of product development, perhaps only the basic principles have been addressed here and further development programmes will each take individual aspects the next step forward. Largely because few organizations yet fully utilize principles such as continuous learning, enhanced out-sourcing of skills, virtual R&D, strategic development partnerships and resource alliances, none have been discussed, but as each are adopted by leading manufacturers, their importance for product development generally will gradually become more apparent. In the meantime, encouraging more companies to embrace some of the basic principles addressed within this book is of greater immediate concern.

Index